The S Word

The S Word

A MEMOIR

PAOLINA MILANA

SHE WRITES PRESS

Published 2015
Printed in the United States of America
ISBN: 978-1-63152-927-6
Library of Congress Control Number: 2015931299

For information, address:
She Writes Press
1563 Solano Ave #546
Berkeley, CA 94707

She Writes Press is a division of Spark Point Studio, LLC.

This book is dedicated to anyone who may be keeping secrets.
To children too little to know they warrant a voice.
To teenagers too confused to think they have a choice.
To adults too overwhelmed to do what's right.
And to those of us who have survived crazy and who—
blessed with a little perspective (not to mention nearly a
decade of therapy)—realize we no longer need to stay silent,
and that spilling secrets may just help others
from feeling as if they need to keep theirs.

Author's Note

People and places and events are all real, as true to my memory as possible. In order to preserve anonymity, I have changed the names of most but not all of the individuals in this book, and in some cases, I have also modified identifying details. No composite characters or events were created in writing this book. Some people and events were purposely omitted, but doing so had no impact on the integrity of the story. It is my hope that the truth I share does justice to all those involved and that it is seen as a story of redemption, forgiveness, and hope.

Sinners

The little red light at the top of the confessional turned to green. Somebody came out: a mom-looking lady. She wasn't much taller than I was but was rounder in the middle. Her hair was the same dirty dishwater blond as mine but not nearly as long or curly. She smiled at me. From the look on her face, I could tell she had gotten a prescription for a clean slate: I estimated five Our Fathers and two Hail Marys.

I wondered what my penance would be.

I tried to calm my nerves by carefully scrutinizing the entire line of those who had come to confess, praying for redemption. An old man. Bald. Looking at me looking at him. Another girl. We were probably the same age—fourteen—but she actually looked the part. I folded my arms across my growing chest.

I tried to assess what had brought them to the box to tell God's chosen servant what they could not keep locked inside their own souls. Were they liars? Thieves? Adulterers? They all looked pretty normal to me. Did I look normal to them? Was my normal the same as theirs? Could they see what my *mamma* must have seen in me so clearly? Could they see why I was there? Could they see the real me?

Another somebody went in. The green light turned to red. Only one booth open to hear confessions today. Lots of sinners waiting. St. Peter's obviously hadn't banked on there being so many. But what did I know? Maybe it was always like this. I hadn't been to Mass in I couldn't remember how long. "Bless me, Father, for I have sinned; it's been _____ since my last confession." At least I remembered my opening line. How long *had* it been?

I thought about it while hopping from one foot to the other, trying *not* to think about how much I needed to go pee. Mass was either on Saturday night or Sunday morning/early afternoon. My hours at the donut shop where I worked were Friday and Saturday from 3:00 p.m. until 11:30 p.m. and Sunday from 7:00 a.m. until 3:30 p.m. Attending Mass was not really an option. So it must have been ever since I'd started working at the donut shop. A year? Maybe closer to two?

I had forged my birth certificate as soon as I'd turned thirteen. Another thing to confess, I guess. I knew it was illegal to do it when I did it, but I didn't really have a choice. I needed a job. My family needed me to need a job. To get one. And part of me wanted one.

I used my uncle Joe's old Olivetti to do it—a breadbox-size steel typewriter that I was convinced had experienced its past life as a blacksmith's anvil. When I typed out the "62" in standard Courier font, the keys almost refused to conspire, causing me to force them into submission not with a finger but with a fist. I whipped the freshly printed paper up and out, but rather than use scissors to cut out my newly minted birth year, I carefully tore around the number. I didn't use glue or any formal adhesive. Spit was all I had to work with. A bit on my index finger applied to the back of the sequin-size gem, the quickest of flips before the paper absorbed too much moisture and the ink began to bleed, a bit of massaging into place so that the "19" lined up and the "65" underneath vanished, and, ta-da! I had grown three years in a matter of moments. A few passes through the lightest setting on the copier, and no one would guess it was a fake.

I took a copy of my new proof of age to the twenty-four-hour donut shop, where a sign taped to the front door beckoned HELP WANTED. I had outgrown my babysitting gigs as much as I had outgrown training bras. I had developed early and passed easily for sixteen—at least. Nobody questioned it.

Red light turned to green again. We had just fifteen minutes left until the start of the Saturday 5:00 p.m. Mass. I could barely keep still, fearful that we would run out of time just as I entered that dark little closet. Somebody else went in. Green light turned to red. One more person after that, and the next would be me. Thank God! Too much time to think was making me think too much.

I shut my eyes and leaned against the church's wood-paneled wall—so smooth, so cool, against my cheek. Mr. Kumar, the donut shop's owner, came to mind again, looking me up and down, literally licking his lips. No taller than the third rack up of donuts on display, he had chocolate-colored skin that oozed as if coated in some sort of donut glaze, and the near-overpowering scent of him made him seem infused with a cumin-like spice. How slippery he looked, sounded. Some bottled water has that same oil-slick sensation. Every time I taste it, it takes me back.

"You work weekend?" he snorted loudly, drawing to the back of his throat what I imagined was accumulated phlegm. He swallowed. "Come."

He led me to the back room, where freshly baked donuts dried on metal racks that rose out from the floor and reached more than halfway to the ceiling. Plain crullers, old-fashioned cake, buttermilk balls, and yet-to-be-filled jelly donuts all waited their turns to be put on display, to be seen, to tempt, and to be chosen by those hungry for a sweet treat. The aroma—a blend of buttercream and lard—now had me licking my own lips.

Mr. Kumar wound his way to the back office, passing giant fryers filled with hot oil; powder-dusted stainless-steel work tables where the remnants of rolled-out dough sat abandoned; half a dozen plastic vats containing strawberry-, maple-, vanilla-, and chocolate-flavored icings and multicolored sprinkles; and two metal contraptions on the floor, positioned in opposite corners of the room, each illustrated with the silhouette of a long-tailed rat stamped out with a giant red "X."

He jammed his key into the door lock, barely cracking it open. He reached in with one hand and pulled out a clear plastic bag big enough to stuff a body. Filled with orange and pink polka-dotted uniforms, however, it looked like a festive piñata. Again he looked me up and down, then reached into the bag and pulled out my exact size, along with a matching apron and cap. He handed the bundle to me.

"Sunday, seven in morning, you be here." A jerk of his chin, a snort, a toss of the clothes bag back into the darkened office, a turn of the key, and Mr. Kumar was shuffling back out toward the front of the shop. Interview over. I guessed I had gotten the job.

The sinner waiting in line behind me nudged me. I opened my eyes, realizing another somebody had come out. Another one had gone in. We inched forward. Red light. Green light. Red again. It reminded me of a game I used to play. I whispered to myself, "Red Rover, Red Rover, let Dahlia come over."

I loved Red Rover. Or Ghosts in the Graveyard. Dahlia—Dahlia Cohen—was a neighbor girl a couple of years older than I was. She played Red Rover with us only once, I think. I wished she would play with us more often. But she preferred playing with boys, so Ghosts in the Graveyard was a game more her speed because when we ran around at night, if the boys caught you, you got kissed. I do confess that I sort of liked that game, too, but I really did try never to get caught. I was too afraid of what would happen if I did.

Dahlia seemed to know everything, including just the right thing to say or do to get what you wanted or to stop what you didn't. She was so lucky. She was Jewish; pretty much everyone in Skokie was Jewish. Except us. I'm pretty sure we were the only Sicilian Catholic family in the village, including Papà and Mamma; Caterina (Cathy), my older sister by five years; Rosario (Ross), the only boy in the family, two years my senior; and Vincenzina (Viny), my little sister by two years. And, of course, there was me: Paolina.

I was my *papà*'s favorite, even though I wasn't the oldest or the baby or even the only boy. He called me *la piccola mamma*, "little mother," a title I earned and willingly stepped into when my age first turned to double digits. The associated job duties—making the morning coffee, making lunches, making dinners; making sure Viny did her homework and took a bath at night; sitting at the kitchen table with Papà as he calculated our weekly spend against his weekly paycheck; translating and writing letters to bill collectors, doctors, schoolteachers, and more; making sure the house was at least picked up, if not clean; and helping make ends meet when needed, be it via babysitting money or via money from the donut shop—came rather easily to me and were necessary in order for Papà to manage our family of six, especially as Mamma was getting sick in her brain, and getting sicker by the minute.

You would think that my older sister, Caterina, would have taken on that role. Sometimes I thought that, too, especially when I was too tired to do it or was just sick of doing it, like all the times I'd have to help my little sister with her homework, even though I had already finished mine and would rather just watch TV. But Cathy wasn't the type. The most she did to help out was start working at the local dry cleaner's at age fifteen. And she wasn't too happy about that. She never seemed too happy about anything. She spent most of her time looking at herself in the mirror, either admiring her model-like body and wondering why she didn't have any boyfriends or brooding about the nose she'd inherited from our *papà* and blaming it for why she didn't. She always seemed bothered by somebody or something. As Papà often said, she always acted as if she had been *morsicata dalle vespe* (stung by wasps).

You might wonder why my older brother, Rosario, wasn't put in charge. He was, I guess, in a way. Being a boy in a Sicilian family, and especially being the only boy, pretty much meant he ruled. Special privileges included telling his sisters what to do but not really having to do anything himself, like pick up his clothes or wash dishes. Besides, at age fifteen, Ross was made a manager at the McDonald's where he worked, so he contributed more financially to the family, and that just added to his status as king. He, too, inherited our *papà*'s Roman nose, but on his face, it fit. At least, all the girls seemed to think so.

Vincenzina was the littlest. Nobody expected her to do much of anything. And when Mamma wasn't sleeping, Mamma pretty much babied her. Even when Viny tried to do things herself, like tie her own shoes, Mamma would grab her feet and do it for her. Sometimes I thought she did it because she didn't want her baby to grow up, but more times than not, I didn't know why Mamma did what she did. And I tried not to think about it.

What I knew for sure was that Papà needed me and I was Daddy's little girl, always aiming to please—him most of all. In some ways, too, I also knew that this role gave me power in the family. And that part, I liked.

The little red light hadn't changed in a long while. What in the world was taking so long? I had to get in there. If I missed my chance at confession today, I didn't know when I'd be able to come back. Mr. Kumar had been pretty clear that if I wanted another weekend day off, I might as well not come back.

A couple of people at the end of the line decided to give up. I guess they figured their sins weren't so bad. They could wait another week for absolution. I could not. At least I didn't think so.

I silently prayed to Jesus: *Red light, green light, red light . . . Jesus, please hurry up and change that light to green.*

I thought about Dahlia again. And about living among the Jews. It was okay with me. I actually wished I were Jewish. Probably not the smartest thing to think while in church, standing in line to talk to Him, or at least His representative, but it was how I felt.

Jewish people didn't have to confess and get absolution. I'm sure Dahlia didn't. And they seemed to have more of everything—more than we did, that's for sure.

While we lived among them, we lived in a house we really couldn't afford. I remember my *papà* saying on moving day, "*Chi sa se la possiamo pagare?*" His question—"Who knows if we can pay for it?"—had me questioning to myself, *Then why are we moving?*

It wasn't a big place: a ranch-style, beige brick three-bedroom with an office on the far end for Mamma's sewing business, and an attached two-car garage—our first. It sat on a corner lot, and—unlike our previous home, which had a giant yard for children to play in—this home on Kedvale had no more than a square five-foot patch of dead grass on the side. Barely enough for Papà's vegetable garden.

When I was old enough to ask and to actually get an answer, Papà told me that he chose to live among the Jews because they ate just as well as Italians and valued family just as much as Italians, but didn't have to fear organized crime the way Italians did. The Mafia was one of the reasons my father left his *bella Sicilia*, a little seaside town on the western coast called Custonaci. As he summed it up: *Meglio partire che morire.* Better to leave than to die.

Of course, as I learned later on from my *papà*'s stories about his restless, playboy spirit and lack of desire to run the family bakery, it was quite possible the Mafia wasn't the only thing my father sought to escape.

Sometimes I wished I could escape. I wished I could be Dahlia, or at least have a cool name like hers; it always sounded so flowery and flirty and pretty. The teachers at school couldn't pronounce my real name, Paolina, so they started calling me Paula; every time I heard that name, I cringed at how much uglier it made me feel. Dahlia got everything she wanted: Gloria Vanderbilt jeans; purple eye shadow. She even had a feather boa. If she cried and yelled, she got more. And she never had to pay for what she wanted, not on her own.

Dahlia was my friend. And she was the first person who told me how babies are made. She told me when I was ten. I just knew she had to be lying. I found out she wasn't when I told my *mamma* what she said and I got slapped. I didn't question it again.

The whole thought of it grossed me out, which is ironic, given that I had already started masturbating by then. I didn't know that was what it was called, that it even had an official name. I just knew that what I was doing felt good. I must not have connected the pleasure of doing it with the penis-in-vagina activity Dahlia had explained to me. Unfortunately, my *mamma* did. She caught me in the act one day. This time, I wasn't just slapped; I was hit. Repeatedly.

But that didn't hurt as much as her berating me. She made fun of what she saw, mimicking my hand movements and facial expressions. I was shocked at first, because I didn't know I even made those facial expressions. I didn't know *anybody* made those facial expressions. I mean, it wasn't like I had yet seen any dirty movies. In truth, I don't know how I even came to touch myself in the first place. I didn't even know it was considered a bad thing.

Well, maybe that's a lie. I must have known, because otherwise I would have been doing it out in the open. I guess maybe I didn't realize that it wasn't something a ten-year-old should be doing. But I already had gotten my period. I got that while babysitting for a set of two-year-old twins. I didn't really know what to do when I realized I was bleeding. Tears erupted, and I called home. My *papà* answered, half-asleep, but the second I started telling him what was happening, he woke up fast and passed the phone to Mamma, who said, "*Non è niente; vieni a casa.*"

Mamma may have thought it was nothing and that I should just come home, but it sure was something to me.

When Mrs. Weiner, the twins' mom, came home and saw the state I was in, she explained it all to me. She showed me how to use a sanitary napkin. She wiped away my tears and said, "Sweetie, it's not nothing; it's a very big something we should celebrate." She said that on Saturday, the next time I was scheduled to babysit, she would take us all out to IHOP for a pancake breakfast. I had never been to IHOP. Mrs. Weiner couldn't believe it. Neither could I.

A little while later, she gave me a book to read: Judy Blume's *Forever*. I read it over and over. And made sure to keep it hidden, and to never again get caught in the act that I could not stop doing.

I didn't think if Mrs. Weiner were my mom and had caught me masturbating that she would have made me feel so ashamed. I thought she and Dahlia's mom would have thought I was normal. Doing normal things. But my *mamma* wasn't raised that way. And on top of that, she didn't think normal thoughts. And while I know now that it wasn't her fault, just as much as it wasn't mine, I sadly didn't know it then. So the best I could do was try to survive, and I did that by trying to keep my distance. Problem was, I wasn't too sure from what or whom I was to keep distant. Especially when wherever I went or with whomever I went, I always brought me with me. And *that* seemed to be the problem.

Finally! With five minutes to spare, the red light turned to green as one more sinner exited the confessional and one more entered: me. I silently thanked Jesus for getting me in on time. I shut the door behind me, imagining the green light turning to red outside. I knelt down on the sparse pad. A chill wrapped itself around me. It smelled so cold, like that time the air conditioner went out in my *papà*'s car and ghostly fumes came out of the vents.

Whenever I was in the confessional, I wondered if this was how it felt to be sealed in a coffin—an ornately carved mahogany coffin, standing up.

The little square screen in front of me slid open. "May the Lord be in our hearts to help you make a good confession."

The voice belonged to Father Tierney. Old-school Father Tierney.

Older-than-the-school Father Tierney. I was not a fan of Father Tierney.

"Bless me, Father, for I have sinned. It's been about a year or so since my last confession."

I waited—for what, exactly, I don't know. But whatever it was, it didn't come. I took a deep breath. I was ready. I opened my mouth to speak. But I needed to build up my courage to say what I had really come to say, so I started out with the amateur stuff: not honoring my mother and father, not always telling the truth, not going to church on Sundays, not being so very nice to my little sis—

"Not going to church on Sundays?" Father Tierney interrupted.

"Pardon me, Father?"

"Why haven't you been going to Sunday Mass? What possible reason could there be to not keep the Lord's Day holy?"

Part of me thought this was a test. Or a trick question. "Well, Father, I . . . I have to work on Saturdays and Sundays. My shift—"

"Nothing could be more important." His voice trembled, because of age or anger, I wasn't sure. "Nothing!"

"But, Father . . ." Either nervous or incredulous, I nearly started laughing. "Father, I can't—"

"Promise me you will come to Mass next Sunday." The church organ started to play some ominous tune.

I paused for a moment, not really knowing what to say. "Father, I already know I'm on the schedule for next week. I can't promise you, because I'd be lying."

"Promise me you will come to Mass next Sunday." Father Tierney's voice grew louder. "*Promise.*"

"But I'd be lying."

"Promise me, or I will not absolve you of your sins." His voice was so loud now, I was certain anybody standing outside could hear. And my heart sank with the realization that he was serious, and I was in trouble.

My voice became very small. "Wait. No. Father, you don't understand. I have to tell you. Please let me tell—"

"If you're not willing to commit to being at Mass next Sunday, I cannot absolve you of your sins." The little screen to salvation slid shut.

I stared at what had been a window of lacy light. I listened to the pipes playing and the people singing outside my door. I could hear Father Tierney breathing. I wanted to tell him. I needed to tell him. I whispered, more to myself than to anyone there, "Father? Please . . ."

The man behind the screen clumsily moved about his box and exited the confessional.

I remained in that box. Alone.

The processional hymn ended, and some other holy man began to speak. I heard the faithful respond with a chorus of "amen"—a word that means "I believe."

As I rose to leave, all I could think was that I no longer did.

I thought that people who loved you weren't supposed to hit or make fun of you. I thought that people who cared for you or who were to act sort of like your adult guardians weren't supposed to touch you, not like that. Or hurt you. Down there. And I thought that people who were to forgive you weren't supposed to deny you absolution, damning you to hell forever.

I had needed to tell. Someone. Anyone. I had needed just one somebody to listen. To hear me. To understand what I could not. To tell me it wasn't my fault. That I wasn't to blame. And then I needed that somebody to pretend I had never said a word. To act as if it had never happened. I needed someone else to be the one who kept this secret so that I could be free of it, washed clean of it. And no one else would be hurt as a result of it.

In 1979, I needed to be a kid again.

Sicilians

Keeping secrets came pretty easily to me. Nobody, not even my friends, knew what was wrong with Mamma or why I had to get a job. Nobody asked. And I was taught early on never to offer information unless I had to, and never, ever to be in anyone's debt. I'm not sure if it was a Sicilian thing, à la *The Godfather* and Cosa Nostra—as in "keep it inside the family" and "none of your business"—or simply an extension of Mamma's SOP of keeping secrets locked inside. Whatever it was, I did it. And I did it well.

I was three years underage when I showed up for my first day at the donut shop, and determined that no one would ever suspect it.

"You ever make a pot o' coffee, girl?"

Karen was one of two ladies Mr. Kumar had told to train me. Aurora was the other. The two were as different as night and day: the former, a practical mom of five in her thirties, pencil-thin, with skin so black it seemed to shine with its own beautiful blue tint, no other makeup needed; the latter, a thickly German-accented, fifty-something, curvaceous sexpot with skin the color of white icing, her face purposely made even whiter so as to be the perfect blank canvas for the palette of colors she artistically applied.

"Yes, ma'am," I said. Inside, I laughed at Karen's question. At thirteen, I was a pro at brewing and drinking the best cups of joe. I immediately felt confident enough to wave good-bye to my *papà*, who, standing among the other twenty or so people—they waiting to be served; he waiting to make sure I was okay—looked anything but ready to leave me there.

He had woken me up before the sun had even risen that Sunday for my first day on the job. He'd whispered in my ear, "Paoletta, è l'ora di lavorare. Faccio il café?"

I had stretched, still clinging to sleep but well aware of my papà's tactic for getting me out of bed: threatening to make the coffee always got me on my feet. I was the best at it, and he and I both knew it.

"I ain't old enough for you to be 'ma'am'-in' me, now," Karen said.

"Ah! You leave her be, Karen. Come over to Aurora, dahlink. Aurora be better teacher."

"That's 'cause you be so much older, wiser," Karen sassed, as she gave me a theatrical shove toward her friend. Aurora, the only one among us to be dressed not in uniform but in what I would learn was her trademark top-cut-too-low-and-skirt-hemmed-too-high substitute, outstretched her arms, not to welcome me to her but to show herself off to the packed house, shaking what she had to shake, literally on cue with Barry Manilow singing on the radio about Lola and her dress cut down to there.

"You should be so lucky to look this good when you're my age! Eat your heart out, eh?" Aurora danced the length of the counter, tip jar in hand.

The crowd laughed and handed over their change, as if at some sort of live show. I was loving it.

"You Paolina's papa?" Karen shouted out to my papà.

Papà beamed, nodding and calling back, "She good girl."

"Your papa is a very handsome man," Aurora commented loudly, winking in his direction. "You married?"

Again the rumble of laughter, the loudest coming from my papà. He had been handsome in his youth. He'd known it and used it, too. Now, looking more like a grandpa than like a Don Juan, he was still a ladies' man—bald head, gap-toothed grin, and all.

"Don't you worry, Papa," Karen interjected. "We'll take good care of your good girl."

"Tank you, miss. I be back for she tree o'clock." Papà had trouble pronouncing "th"; we practiced and practiced, but he just couldn't get his tongue, the roof of this mouth, and the back of his teeth to work together to form the sound that didn't exist in Italian. Still, everyone knew what he meant, and everyone joined in bidding him farewell, at Karen's lead.

"Bye, Paolina's papa!"

As my father exited, two police offers entered. It was the first time I'd noticed the little bells attached to the top hinges of the door. They chimed to announce the arrival of newcomers.

"Lesson one," Karen was suddenly whispering in my ear. "Always give the cops freebies. Whatever they ask for. You hear? That way, you stay safe."

I nodded, taking her words to heart but having no clue whatso ever how true, and how devastating, they would come to be for me. She left to attend to the men whose job it was "to serve and protect."

Patrons waiting for their morning treats occupied every pink stool along the white Formica counter shaped in some serpentine fashion. We stood between them and stainless-steel coffeemakers, refrigerators, and rows and rows of white ceramic cups, saucers, and little plates. At one end of the counter, the one that led to the back room where the donuts were made, a low glass case featuring specialty donuts, including the newest jelly- and cream-filled donut holes, supported the cash register. Behind it sat row upon row of fresh donuts just begging to be eaten. And at the very top of those racks beamed a milk-glass, almost see-through sign listing all the tasty options and prices.

"Okay, you see this?" Aurora held out a glass coffee decanter, seemingly burned at the bottom. "You think there is no hope, yes?"

I really didn't think much of anything, but I nodded.

"You watch." Aurora went to the freezer and scooped up some ice cubes. She tossed them into the decanter. She then put a scoop of kitchen cleanser in. Then just a dribble of water. And vigorously—her whole body shaking (more than it needed to)—shook that decanter until the scorched bottom was scrubbed crystal clear. She held it out for all to see. And those who did applauded.

On that first day, I learned how to properly pack a dozen donuts, especially when the frosting was still wet, so that it wouldn't rub off on other donuts; how to work the machines, including the coffee-maker, which had a tendency to get blocked, not drip, and overflow from the top, where the grinds were; how to clean glass decanters that looked scorched beyond salvation; and, most important, how to serve customers, whether you liked them or not, and how to work a room, mostly to get bigger tips. And at all of it, I proved to be a natural.

My *papà* returned at three o'clock, as promised. He'd come back early to sit and watch me work my final thirty minutes.

"Look, Papà!" I held out my tip jar. Instant money. "All for me!"

Karen eased the jar from my hands. "Not all for you, hon. We split—you, me, and Aurora. Boss said you'd be workin' Friday and Saturday nights alone. Then it can be all for you."

I gave my *papà* a free cup of coffee and a donut. "*Brava!*" he said as he bit down on a honey glazed, still warm and wet.

Karen whispered in my ear again, "And don't let Kumar see you doin' that. You can. Just make sure he don't see it."

I nodded.

"Your girl done good, Papa," Karen said. She put on her jacket and pocketed her tips.

Aurora came, took hers, and gave me a big kiss. "Ach! To be so young again!" She leaned over the counter, her breasts nearly spilling out of her top, and kissed my *papà*, too. "Good job with your good girl, Papa."

Papà paid me to pack a dozen donuts to take home. I made sure Mr. Kumar was watching. Mamma wasn't feeling well. Her favorites were Boston creams: chocolate on top with custard in the middle. I made sure to include two, hoping they would make her happy. Ross's favorites were raspberry jelly–filled and white-iced long johns. Cathy loved double chocolates. Viny always wanted sprinkles. Papà and I were partial to French crullers and buttermilk balls. I made sure to pick only the freshest. I had learned that day that pink paper in the morning meant they were just baked, but pink paper in the afternoon meant they were the older ones. I chose only those on white paper.

When we got home, everyone surrounded me, each grabbing for his or her favorite treat. Everyone except Mamma. She was in bed. Again.

I put a Boston cream on a small plate and took it to her, climbing the five or six stairs that led from the kitchen to my parents' bedroom.

The drapes were drawn. It was so dark. She had made those drapes herself, when she wasn't sick. They were a hunter green, with accents of gold to match Mamma's bedspread.

She lay there, covers held tightly around her head. It always hurt her so much, but no one could figure out why.

"Mamma," I whispered, "*alzarti. Veni a mangiare.*" I showed her the Boston cream. "*Guarda. C'è la crema dentro.*"

Mamma poked her head out from the covers, her face a bloated marshmallow. She looked at the donut and then at me and tried to smile. "*Paoletta mia. Grazie. Ma non ora. Più tarde. Non ora.*" She turned away from me, covering her head again.

Even enticing Mamma to get up and come eat, tempting her with a cream-filled donut, her favorite, didn't work. "Not now" and "later" had become answers to bet on.

But she hadn't always been this way.

When I was nine, Mamma enrolled me in ballet. Mrs. Regan, an old, wrinkly ballerina wannabe who lived within walking distance and who taught ballet and tap in her home, became my teacher. I never really wanted to learn to dance, but Mamma had never been allowed to dance, period, when she was little, so it became very important to her that I did. And I did not want to disappoint.

Things Mamma worked so hard to give me early on—like the ballet lessons—would end up being among the very things she pointed to as evidence of my bad behavior later. I never really understood it back then. I figured she just changed her mind or that it was my fault.

It sure would have helped to know that what was happening to her had very little, if anything, to do with me, and most, if not everything, to do with the voices in her head she could no longer control. Then again, I'm not sure how, as a nine-year-old, I would have handled knowing that voices were telling my mother that she should kill me. In hindsight, maybe it was best to just think I was a bad girl who attracted all sorts of evil and could do no right. Maybe.

Mrs. Regan carried a big stick, sort of like a semiflexible cane, that doubled as a walker and a whip. She used it to hit those of us who couldn't get our little bodies to pose appropriately. I was a favorite target of hers. Not sure why. The backs of my legs bore witness to my lack of grace or my inability to force my feet into first or fifth position. Or, more likely, it was because I liked to laugh. I just found things funny. Like when my leg got stuck in between the wall and the barre and I needed one of the other little girls to unstick me. I couldn't help being so short. We all dissolved into giggles. Except Mrs. Regan. And we grew silent pretty quickly as soon as that stick struck one of us, usually me.

"Miss Milana, what *is* so funny?"

"Miss Milana, I said feet in fourth, not fifth!"

On this particular day, in Mrs. Regan's cold, concrete basement, void of any windows, I had placed my hand on the barre, as ordered, and a spider had come out of a hole and crawled onto me, so I'd screamed like a little girl—a perfectly acceptable reaction, I would think, given the fact that that is exactly what I was.

Whack! Mrs. Regan's stick caught my forearm as she began to scream at me. Something about me causing another disruption, and something about her not needing someone like me, and finally something about me getting my things and getting out. Now!

I had been kicked out of class.

The odd part? Even back then, some small part of me knew Mrs. Regan would regret her decision. After all, I was the only dancer who didn't even need toe shoes to pirouette on the very tippy-tops of my feet. And I was the chosen star of her upcoming spring showcase. Mrs. Regan must have forgotten. I sure as hell hadn't.

I ran home and sobbed into my *mamma*'s arms, begging her not to make me go back. She rocked me and kept saying, over and over, "Okay, no cry, no cry." Sometimes it was warm and wonderful being Mamma's daughter back then, back before she started hearing voices.

The next time we were scheduled to have dance class, I was a no-show. Mrs. Regan called Mamma to tell her that all was forgiven and that I would be allowed to return. I remember Mamma's face as she held the receiver to her ear; I could see her growing rage, just waiting to be unleashed. A few moments into the call, Mamma mustered her best English to tell Mrs. Regan to go to hell. I could not have beamed more proudly. But even then, as much as I was thrilled to have been given such a get-out-of-jail-free card, I knew that it must have killed Mamma to give up on yet another of her dreams. When she hung up the phone and I hugged her, her smile was a show for me, but she couldn't hide her moist eyes. In that moment, I wished I had not screamed at that spider.

Mamma's own mother and father died before she even made it out of her teens. She was the youngest female in a very strict Sicilian household, and so her eldest brother, our Uncle Joe, became her appointed caretaker. She would follow him to America, even if she didn't want to and even if it meant leaving everyone and everything she knew back in her hometown, the landlocked central Sicilian city of Nicosia.

Mamma was a talented seamstress—so talented that when she emigrated to the United States at the age of thirty-one, in 1958, the famous designer Emilio Pucci commissioned her to sew for him. She was also beautiful. When my *papà*, a self-made barber ten years her senior, was on a ship heading toward his own American dream, he befriended Mamma's younger brother, Salvatore (Sam), who showed Papà a photo of his still-single sister—Mamma in her twenties—dressed as a mandolin player in celebration of Carnivale. My father loved playing *il mandolino*, and when he saw my mother, with hair the color of ravens' feathers, skin as smooth and creamy as a home-made zabaglione, blood-red lipstick—her signature—and curves that filled out that mandolin player's costume, to hear him tell it, he was hit by "the thunderbolt," just like *The Godfather*'s Michael Corleone when he first laid eyes on his Apollonia.

For Mamma, I would learn much later in life, it wasn't so much love at first sight as it was her biological clock ticking too loudly. That, and she did confess a fondness for Papà's bald head. Oh, and she thought, because of the way he dressed, that he was rich (an assumption that proved false, very false). And she wanted to break free from living under the thumb of her eldest brother, my Uncle Joe.

I guess when it came down to it, everyone wanted to escape from something, somewhere, someone. Sometimes, maybe, even to escape from themselves. I guessed that was how Mamma felt. I knew that was how I felt.

Ross said everybody wants to get away. That's what he said my pet goldfish, Bubbles, wanted. I was in the third grade when I got the fish. I won him at some local fair. Threw a Ping-Pong ball into his fishbowl and probably scared him near to death. He was fat, with bulging eyes and a bulbous body with swirls of orange, white, and red. He reminded me of rainbow sherbet.

Every morning, it was my job to feed him. I would head for the downstairs bathroom to pee and to give him just a pinch of fish flakes, no more, no less. Otherwise, Ross told me, Bubbles might explode. But on this one day when I entered the room, Bubbles was gone. His little round glass bowl, still full of water, was missing him. I looked around, not noticing where I was walking, until I felt something rubbery under my toes. Luckily, I hadn't actually stepped on Bubbles and squashed him. Then again, it wouldn't have mattered. As he lay on the cold tile floor, a dribble of water trailing around him, I realized he was already dead.

My one and only pet, my first, had committed suicide.

As Ross surmised, "He'd do anything to get away from you."

I shook the picture of Bubbles free from my mind. I placed the Boston cream on Mamma's nightstand.

"*Più tarde, Mamma. Dormi.*" I could do nothing more for her than to tell her to sleep. Later, she could eat her treat.

I slowly walked out of her bedroom. I couldn't help but wish things were different. How much I wanted her to come alive again. To hold me like she had when I was more important than even ballet classes. How much I wanted to share with her how my first day at the donut shop had gone, and how I couldn't wait to go back: to work behind the counter, to learn how to make the donuts, to serve all those people, and to be faster and funnier than Karen or even Aurora. I wanted to perform, like they did. I wanted to have people applauding my moves and to get lots of tips because of it. I wanted my *mamma* to come see me in action, to see the real me, and to say that she thought I was great. Or at least for her to recognize that I was normal.

I counted the days until I could return to the donut shop, until I could be free to be me again. I dreamed of being something big and this being just the start of it. I wished for what I wanted, not realizing then what it would mean when I actually got it.

Strawberries

On my first Friday night, I was going to be working solo. I couldn't wait to change out of my blue plaid school-issued jumper and into my pink polka-dotted donut-shop uniform, but getting out of school in time to do it proved tricky. I couldn't let the teachers know about my job, because that would be the end of my donut-diva career, so I had to practically sneak out of Mr. Olenstek's last-period science class to catch the bus. I didn't even have enough time to say "Have a nice weekend" to him.

Mr. Olenstek wasn't a regular teacher. He had a mustache. And he wore tight corduroys. He was funny, too. And I thought about him. A lot. About as much as I did about Father Francis P. Murphy, who looked nothing like a priest but like one of those male models in a magazine who showed off his underwear. Or at least that's what I thought he would look like under that collared robe. He also was cool enough to have a real pinball machine in his bedroom. He let some of us play with it once, but that was supposed to be our secret, too. He looked and acted more like a kid, more like one of us. I couldn't get him out of my head. I even dreaded going to Mass when he was there, because of all the thoughts I knew I shouldn't be thinking.

I made my way to the donut shop and quickly learned that Friday nights working solo were quite a bit different from Sunday mornings. At least on this Friday, practically no one showed up. There was no one to perform for. No customers to collect tips from. No one to talk to. I was all alone. My only companion, the radio, kept me company. I loved the songs. Loved the words. And while I hoped that this silent Friday wasn't typical, I found myself loving being able to retreat into a world of my own, where it was safe to sing out loud and dance and just be me.

"You Make Me Feel Like Dancing" . . . I danced and thought about regular stuff, like school and homework. "Kiss You All Over" . . . I danced and thought about my friends or the cute boys in my classes. "Hot Child in the City" . . . Sometimes I allowed myself to think about Mr. Olenstek or Father Murphy or even some of the dads of the kids I babysat. And I tried not to think about all those other things, things that Mamma said were wrong. Things that weren't normal. About me.

Maybe she was right. Maybe something *was* wrong with me, because I couldn't stop thinking about boys. I don't think she knew I thought about boys who were no longer boys, but I'm pretty sure she would have thought it wrong as well—most likely worse than wrong. But as long as she wasn't around, I thought about them; I couldn't help it. And I made sure to crank up the music and sing and dance around to my favorites, especially songs from Styx's *Grand Illusion.*

Styx's album came out in 1977, and Ross and Cathy actually took me to see their live concert at the Rosemont Horizon for my twelfth birthday. We sat on the main floor in folding chairs. I got to stand on my chair and sing as loud as I wanted to, and shake my behind and just go crazy! It felt wonderful to feel so free, to have nobody watching and condemning things I thought just had to be normal— for example, my brother, Ross, holding my hand so I wouldn't fall. Mamma wouldn't have approved. But she wasn't there, so I could just be me.

I think that's why I loved Styx so much. That concert was my very first, and was one of the very few times in my life up to that point when I could enjoy being *normal,* or at least what I thought normal to be. I think that's also why I made sure always to sing out loud to any Styx tune whenever one played on the radio. And that was exactly what I was doing when I was all alone at the donut shop, belting out my best "Fooling Yourself":

"Blow, blow, blow, blow . . . Bloooowwwwwwwoooo . . ." *Uh-oh.*

My singing was interrupted when a man entered the donut shop.

This man came out of nowhere. No car in the parking lot. No headlights to signal a patron's arrival. I couldn't even remember hearing the tinkling bells of the door opening when he walked in. But, like I said, I was singing out loud, so maybe I missed it. All I know is that I turned around and he was there. Pacing. Back and forth. Back and forth. Back and forth, the entire length of the shop. Only his pacing was more of a shuffle.

The only thing between the man and me was the counter.

Fear shot through me. For a moment, I became paralyzed. And at the same moment, he stopped moving and turned to face me. We stared at each other, me sweating, the man expressionless.

He was an older fellow, older than my *papà*. And fatter by about seventy-five pounds. And taller. For sure, he was a good six inches taller than I was. Or maybe he just seemed bigger because I felt so very alone and small. His hair was wispy and seemed to be in a permanent state of attention, yet each strand was saluting its own captain. His plain gray-but-used-to-be-white T-shirt was stained with remnants of meals from days gone by. He sported nearly worn-through pajama bottoms with faded blue stripes, and on his feet were tattered brown slippers. The slushy gray snow still on the ground had soaked through them and the bottoms of his pants. He reminded me of a used washrag.

I found the courage to stammer out, "Can I help you?"

He started to pace/shuffle again. It was then that I noticed his wristband. A hospital wristband. I knew what I was looking at. And while I was still very much afraid, a strange sense of comfort came over me. *I've been here before,* I thought. *With Mamma.* And I knew I had to get help.

Too bad Mr. Kumar had disabled the phone from dialing out. I'm sure it was illegal. I had a sense from day one that a lot of what Mr. Kumar did was probably illegal. Lucky for me, Karen had shown me how to make an outgoing call, even though the rotary-style dialer no longer functioned.

I dialed 911 by depressing the switch hook (the part of the phone that the handpiece sits on to hang it up) very fast as many times as it took to dial each digit. So I quickly tapped it nine times, then waited, then one time, then waited, then one time again. The call went through.

Moments later, two officers showed up. They introduced themselves. Officer James Brown. Officer Tim Gunner. Both seemed to be the same age: late thirties or early forties.

Officer Brown was black, with skin several shades lighter than Karen's, and his uniform showed off every muscle. He had a lot of them. He told some funny jokes, and his smile never left his lips. He said he had a couple of kids. And he loved the plain old-fashioned donuts. He said he was telling me that because I was the new girl. I made a mental note to give him a couple before he left.

Officer Gunner towered at a slender but muscular six feet. He had strawberry-blond hair, the bluest of eyes, the most Cheshire Cat–like smile, and the swagger of a "been around the block and I carry a gun" Clint Eastwood.

I loved Clint Eastwood. Papà and I regularly sat up late nights to watch him in movies, especially in his Westerns. *The Man with No Name* was the last one we had seen; Papà loved it. So did I, but my favorite was still *The Outlaw Josey Wales*.

Everything was taken from Josey: his home, his wife, his son. For no reason. He didn't deserve any of it. Josey could've given up, but he didn't. He fought back. He found a whole new family, sort of—a bunch of misfits from some ghost town he was passing through. He saved them all. He saved himself. And he saved a young girl from getting raped by a bunch of desperados. I think that was my favorite part. That, and how Josey kept spitting out his chewing tobacco onto that poor dog that followed him around everywhere. I always thought that dog should have figured it out after a while and just kept his distance. But he never did.

I watched as Officer Brown and Officer Gunner took charge of the situation. They asked me where the donut-shop owner was or if I knew how to get ahold of him. I didn't.

Soon after, while Officer Brown watched over the man with the hospital bracelet and Officer Gunner called for an ambulance, I saw Officer Gunner brushing some hair off his shirtsleeve. He put his hand over the receiver and sort of whispered to me that he was single and that he had a couple of cats.

I nodded. I liked cats, too.

That's what I told him.

Officers Brown and Gunner spent some more time checking the man out, asking him questions and getting no answers. They put handcuffs on him. The man never said a word. He just kept rocking back and forth but in place.

After a little while, the ambulance came and took him away. Officer Brown went with. Officer Gunner stayed behind.

I never gave another thought to the two men who left.

My thoughts were instantly consumed with Officer Gunner, who, for the first of what would be many times over the course of a year, sat himself down on the first pink stool in front of the curved white counter and ordered a coffee—black, two sugars. And a strawberry-iced raised donut. That first time, I couldn't help but giggle.

"What's so funny?" he asked.

"Nothing. Is this to go?" I had a hard time keeping a straight face. I just kept thinking that this big cop was eating the same donut usually ordered by the little girls who came with their parents to pick out a dozen donuts after church on Sunday mornings.

Had I been paying attention, I might have connected the dots.

"I think I'll have it here. With you."

I served him the donut on a plate and said, "This coffee's been on for a while. I can make a fresh pot." I had one hand on the handle of the basket that held the coffee grinds, ready to yank it out and replace it with freshly ground beans, and casually looked over my shoulder at him. "If you want. Officer Gunner."

He paused a moment longer than I thought was necessary and then uttered two simple words: "I want."

I want. I want. I want. Innocent words on their own, but Officer Gunner's tone and the look on his face made me turn away and blush. I kept my back to him while I busied myself brewing the coffee.

"And, hey, it's just Gunner," he added. "What's your name?"

I answered without turning. "Paolina, but people call me Paula. It's easier."

"Well, *POWwwwleeena, this* is the best donut ever created. Mmm. This is so good."

I couldn't help but turn around and watch as he devoured that donut. *Devoured.*

"Strawberries. My favorite." He licked around his lips and then licked his fingers clean.

So many thoughts and feelings were raging through me. I think the best way to describe it is to say that I was unnerved. By him. By myself. Inside, I felt all jumbly. And I suddenly wanted Officer Gunner—Gunner—gone. And to jump into an ice bath.

I quickly grabbed an empty coffee mug and placed it under the stream of flowing coffee, no longer wanting to wait the additional minutes for a full pot to brew. I turned and placed the steaming cup in front of him, along with a spoon and the sugar dispenser. And then, instinctively, I stepped back. As far as I could. Until my back was up against the refrigerator. I'm not sure why, exactly—especially because part of me wanted to step forward, to cross over the counter, even.

"If you like strawberry, you should try our strawberry jelly–filled donuts," I said, trying to sound—well, professional, I guess, but no doubt sounding like a nervous schoolgirl. Which, in case anybody's missed it, I was. Gunner laughed and took a few gulps of his drink; despite what had to be its scorching temperature, he never flinched.

"Are you always here by yourself, this late at night?" he asked. I couldn't tell if he was concerned or something else. Was this all me? Was I doing it again—whatever it was Mamma said I did? I didn't know what to think. And luckily, at that moment it didn't matter, because just over Gunner's shoulder, I saw Papà's headlights. We had decided on a signal just that morning: he would always flash his headlights three times so I'd know he was there.

"My father," I explained, pointing out the window. "That's him now."

We watched as Papà made his way out of the car and across the parking lot.

I started to stammer, suddenly feeling like a baby rather than a grown-up in charge of the donut shop. "He couldn't come any earlier tonight. He's not a fan of me being here late by myself, so he's come to sit with me. That's what he'll do when he can. That's what he said. Now we just have to wait for one of the bakers to come in, and I can go home."

I don't know why I couldn't stop blabbering so.

Papà pushed open the door of the shop. The tinkling of the bells ushered him in.

"'Look, Daddy, every time a bell rings, an angel gets his wings.'"

Papà and I always stayed up late during Christmastime to watch *It's a Wonderful Life* together. We'd snuggle up close on the couch in the dark. We'd drink Swiss Miss instant hot cocoa—the kind with the little marshmallows, if he remembered to buy it. Otherwise, we'd drink hot tea. Mamma would come out of her bedroom two, three, four times throughout to check up on us, asking us what we were doing. Papà would answer the first, maybe even the second, time. The accusing tone of her voice would escalate. The way she'd look at us made me instinctively inch away, but Papà wouldn't let me move. We'd end up pretty much just ignoring her until she went away, and then both continuing to watch the movie.

Those tinkling angel bells comforted me, reminding me of Clarence finally getting his wings. And my *papà* I cast in the role played by Jimmy Stewart. They were a perfect match: neither really wanting what he ended up with, both the "smartest ones of the bunch" but never quite seeing the smartest moves to make or all the possible ways out.

Papà strode over to the first seat, which Gunner now occupied. Paying him no mind, he continued on to the next stool over. Before sitting down, he leaned over the counter to give me a kiss.

"How my baby girl?"

I couldn't help but smile whenever Papà called me his baby girl. It made me feel like George Bailey's Zuzu: safe and loved, and not as old as I usually felt. And on this night, it made me feel exactly as young as I needed to feel, while at the same time embarrassingly too young to feel like what I wanted to feel: the girl in charge; the girl in control.

"Papà, this is Officer Gunner."

Gunner extended his hand and shook my *papà*'s. "Nice to meet *POWwww*leeena's father. You have a very adult daughter."

Instinct had me practically stumbling over my words to explain to Papà in Italian (English would have taken too long) what Gunner had said and my interpretation of his comment about my being "very adult." I almost felt as if I had to defend myself, my honor. It was crazy. I hadn't done anything. Or I didn't think I had. I wasn't sure anymore. Maybe it was just me. I had no real idea if Gunner meant, "She just had to deal 'like an adult' with an escapee from some mental ward" or if he meant . . . well, something else. I explained the former version to Papà, but something inside me thought Gunner's comment had more to do with the latter.

"Oh, thank you, Ufficiale." Papà charmed even in his broken English. "I know. She be so smart. I work late tonight, so no can be here. But almost all time, I gonna be here. No, Paolina?"

I nodded. I knew how guilty he felt that he hadn't been able to come sit with me on my first solo flight.

"Your name?" asked Gunner.

"Oh, 'scuze me, Ufficiale. My name Antonino, but Tony okay, too."

"Okay. You Tony. Me Tim." We all laughed. "Tony, if you want, I can always drive by and, if you're not here, stop in for a while, make sure I keep an eye on our girl here." Gunner looked right into my eyes, piercing my core. "And *you* can start teaching me to speak Italian."

I looked away.

Papà looked at me. "*Ma che dice?*"

I almost thanked God that Papà had no idea what was being said. And then I almost cursed God that he had no idea what was being said. I explained to Papà in Italian what Gunner was offering. When he understood, he erupted in praise and thanks.

Gunner now officially had permission to keep his eyes on me.

Scissors

When we climbed back into Papà's Pontiac Catalina for the ride home from the donut shop, I tried to look without looking, back over my shoulder, even swinging my book bag a few times, to see if Gunner was still there, still sipping his coffee, still sitting where we'd left him, still waiting for Officer Brown to come back and pick him up, still looking—maybe—at me.

But I couldn't see. Not without totally spinning around and facing him. And that, I thought, would be a mistake, not just if Gunner saw but because I didn't want Papà to know what I was thinking, feeling. It fell under the Sicilian rule of never offering information unless you had to.

As we drove the fifteen minutes or so back home, Papà couldn't stop talking. He practically sang out how proud he was of his baby girl and how even the *ufficiale* could see the specialness in me. He said he knew that in no time I would "eat them up."

"Un giorno, Paolamia, li mangerià!"

I wasn't sure exactly what he meant by that. Whom would I eat? Why would I eat them? How? I didn't bother asking. Instead, I was thinking, *Hey, it was my first day. My first day solo at a job I am three years too young to legally have. And on my first day, I encountered an escapee or a crazy somebody who*—I realized right then in the car—*could easily have taken one of the donut baker's instruments and sliced me open and stuffed me with some of that strawberry jelly before anybody even noticed.*

But I just smiled in response. I let Papà talk. I let him feel proud of a person whom he was responsible for making.

I sat silent during the entire car ride home. At least on the outside. Inside, my thoughts were racing around, smashing into one another, and starting to give me a headache. I didn't know if what I was feeling was pure fear or something else. And I wasn't too sure of what, exactly, I was afraid.

The voices in my own head couldn't come to an agreement, either.

You need to quit.

You can't quit. We need the money.

But you could get hurt.

You just have to be more aware. You know what danger looks like when you see it. Pay more attention!

Listen to how your papà is bragging about you!

"POWwwwleeena . . ."

If I quit, I wouldn't be what Papà thought of me.

If I quit, I might never see Gunner again.

By the same token, somewhere inside me that night, I knew, too, that if I didn't quit, I wouldn't be what Papà thought of me in part because I *would* see Gunner again.

I jerked my head free from the noise, but I could not set myself free from replaying the tapes of what Gunner had said that night. In my mind, I even saw it all again, much as I would have if I'd been sitting in a movie theater, looking up at a giant, glowing screen, its light shining down on me, the characters bringing me to life with every word spoken, every gesture made.

I imagined myself up there on the screen—the damsel in distress, the girl with a heart of gold who had it in her to take care of herself, to fight back all foes, but who, this time, had gotten in a little bit over her head. I watched Gunner as the hero, swooping in to rescue me. Just like Rocky rescued Adrian from her life as a shy, ugly spinster.

"I wanna kiss ya . . . Ya don't have to kiss me back if ya don't feel like it."

That's what he said to her, Rocky to Adrian. When they were alone in his tiny apartment. He cornered her. Wearing just his wife-beater undershirt, he raised his arms, hanging them from a pipe or something that ran parallel to the ceiling. His entire being threatened to swallow her up.

I was only eleven when I first saw *Rocky*, but I felt just like Adrian when I watched that scene, feeling feelings I'd never had before. Not for a real grown-up man.

I swore I could even smell him.

In every sense of the word, Rocky took her. And I watched. Feeling taken, too. And just like Adrian, who was completely changed afterward—new hair, new clothes, new attitude, changed for the better—so, too, was I.

I didn't know at that moment that that wasn't always how it worked. Being taken. And being better.

Just like I didn't know that by the time *Rocky* ended, it would be dark outside. Or that the buses didn't run as often after daytime hours.

I had told Mamma that I was going out that Sunday, but, truth be told, I can't exactly be sure she was actually physically present and listening when I told her. And, to be even more truthful, I'm pretty sure that was all part of my plan.

I wanted to go see *Rocky* with my friend Loretta. I wanted to see it more than I wanted anything else at that moment in my life. And the only way to get to where the movie was playing—the Golf Mill Theaters—was on a couple of buses for at least that many hours. And Mamma wouldn't have approved.

Loretta said not to worry about the late hour; she said once we reached her house, her dad would drive me home and he would smooth things over with my parents.

But when we got to Loretta's house, her mom and dad were in a screaming match. They barely noticed us as we entered and, given the way they were acting, probably didn't even realize their own daughter had been out of the house and missing well into after-curfew hours.

Loretta, her eyes wide with fear, whispered to me, "You better go."

So, all alone, darkness all around, I somehow made it onto a bus that dropped me off just a few blocks from home. By that time, I knew I was in trouble. And I was scared.

Every breeze made the trees swish and sway, the sound like a scratching on a blackboard. The moon cast shadows that looked more like tentacles reaching out to snatch me.

I ran the four blocks from the bus stop to my front door, just in time to see Papà looking gravely concerned and pulling out of the driveway to search for me.

What I did not know at that moment but would learn just moments later was that upon seeing me and learning that I hadn't been murdered, he would decide to beat me until I wished I had been murdered.

I must confess: I would have gone to the movies even if I'd known ahead of time that I would get a severe beating afterward.

Every lash of his belt was worth it.

Rocky was worth it.

Gunner was worth it.

We jerked to a stop. It brought me out of my movie scenes and back to reality.

"*Ecco!*" Papà announced our arrival home.

As I pulled on the passenger-door lever to exit, he gently tapped on my left forearm with his two fingers. With one foot already out the door, I turned my head to face him. He leaned into me, his eyes still expressing praise for his daughter but now looking a bit clouded.

"*La mamma.*" He whispered it, as if in fear of someone's hearing. That was how he always seemed to speak about Mamma, at least lately. Every time he said her name or spoke about her, it was hushed. A secret. One that not even he knew.

I barely listened to what he had to say. I had heard it before:

Mamma had had another bad day; we needed to keep quiet around her; her head hurt worse today than yesterday.

I nodded. I always nodded, whether or not I really understood. It gave my *papà* comfort, courage. Of that I was sure.

He released me, and I made my way through the open garage, traveling into our home, stopping to check if Mamma was in her sewing room, the office room, first on the left. Empty. Two at a time, I took the four little stairs that led up to a tiny landing, then did the same with the four identically little stairs leading down into the laundry room, which also doubled as our second kitchen area, complete with sink, stove, oven, fridge, and freezer. Every good Italian family had two kitchens. And while that fact seemed to surprise the very few friends I ever invited over, what surprised me more were those stairs. I spent more time wondering why my house had those couple of stairs going up to nothing and couple of stairs going down from nothing, with nothing much in the middle. It puzzled me. And no matter how many times I crossed that area, no matter how many times I told myself I wouldn't give it even a single thought, I couldn't help but ponder why whoever built them didn't just make it a flat, connecting hallway. I just couldn't figure out a good enough reason for do—

"*Raaarrrrrrr!*"

"Aaaaah!" I screamed, dropping my book bag and jumping into the air.

Ross jumped out from behind the water heater and nearly fell to the floor in hysterics.

"You jerk!" I tried to punch him, but he bobbed and dove out of the line of fire.

"Paulie, you ain't nothin' but a little girl!" In his finest Rocky Balboa voice, my brother coughed out—in between his body-shaking fits of laughter—his latest adaptation of mashed-up favorite movie lines, the original having said something about Paulie's being "nothin' but a bum." Ross always changed the ending, depending on the situation. But one thing that never changed was his renaming me Paulie.

I hated it. As much as I loved it.

Just as I hated his always jumping out of hiding places to scare me. As much as I loved it.

I was the only one of his sisters whom he teased or with whom he even wanted to spend time. The fact that I had sort of a nickname, and from *Rocky*, to boot, well, it meant something.

Rocky was a favorite movie of Ross's, the man one of his heroes as well, but for different reasons than mine. Ever since Ross had seen the movie, back when he was fourteen, about an underdog who triumphs against all odds, and heard its charging theme song, something had changed in him. He'd become focused, driven, confident. Maybe he was just at the right age for it, but I swear the movie had something to do with it. Plus, for the past couple of years, Ross's fascination with *Rocky* had led him to purchase and use boxing gloves, a punching bag, a speed bag, and I'm not sure what else. And he ran at night: seven-minute miles. I knew they were seven minutes because he took me along the first time. I rode my bicycle behind him. And huffed and puffed just trying to keep up.

It was the first and only time. Mamma found blood in my underwear. Not period blood, either. She kept track of our cycles. When she examined me down there, she said she saw cuts. Cuts that she said were from me touching myself. My fingernails were naturally long. She screamed at me, looked at me with such disgust, I felt what she thought me to be: dirty.

But I hadn't. Touched myself. I knew where the blood and the cuts had come from. Ross knew, too. I had ridden my bicycle into a pothole by accident while riding behind him during his run. The top edge of the seat had some exposed metal that had smashed into my privates. Ross and I thought it best not to say anything. We didn't want Mamma to stop us from running and riding together. I had tried to wash my underwear so that she wouldn't find out. But, obviously, I hadn't done such a great job of it.

I know Ross must have felt awful, standing outside the bathroom door, listening, while I was getting hit. But he knew he couldn't rescue me, and I couldn't tell the truth, so I just kept quiet, wishing that I had been smart enough to throw the underwear away.

A panicked Papà suddenly came barreling through to the laundry room where Ross and I were, the two of us still laughing.

"Che è successo? Dov'è la mamma?"

We froze, instantly reminded that we were supposed to have been quiet. We both scrambled to say that nothing had happened, we were sorry, everything was okay, including Mamma. Papà's face darkened and he stormed off, pretending to still be angry as he left us, stomping through the rest of the house to the upstairs kitchen in search of Mamma.

Ross and I giggled. We couldn't help it.

And then we heard her.

"Se non lo fai tu, Antonino; lo farò da me stesso."

Ross and I raced to reach the sound of our Mamma's voice telling Papà that if he didn't do it, she would do it herself. What "it" was sent my body into prickly convulsions. Because whatever "it" was, I knew it wasn't good.

There she stood, in the center of our downstairs recreation room, right next to the old glass cabinet that housed Papà's barbershop supplies: shaving mugs, soaps, towels, razors, clippers, and sharpening straps. Surrounded by faux wood–paneled walls. Supported by an ugly, scuffed-up brown floor. Able to look out of ground-level windows through which she could see our lawn, the sidewalk, and people walking by—but only from about their knees to their toes.

This was the room where we watched television. The room where we played. The room where we did homework, if the kitchen table was otherwise occupied. The room where Papà sat customers down in an overstuffed olive-green barber chair and trimmed a bit off the top and sides or gave them a shave.

And it would now be the room where my *mamma* would plunge the sharpest of six-inch sewing shears into her head.

"*No, Maria . . . no!*" Papà pleaded.

Mamma began to cry, saying that the only way to get the doctors to look inside her head and take away the pain would be if we gave them a start. She begged Papà to stab her in her skull with the scissors.

I looked at my two sisters, cowering in the corner of the room. Their faces—blank, wide-eyed, stony—told me that they must have had an entire day of this, of Mamma's screams and rants and threats.

It was nothing new. For any of us. But it was getting worse.

I watched the scene unfold, much like a movie: fully invested in what happened to the characters on the screen, yet purposely not allowing myself to feel 100 percent part of the drama, unless I chose to. Remaining removed was my way to survive.

I heard Papà reason with Mamma that he would go to jail if he did what she asked. And who, then, he followed, would look after the children?

A glimmer of logic flashed across Mamma's face. I saw it. And whenever I did, which was less and less often lately, I let go of the breath I did not realize I was holding in.

Carefully, slowly, Papà inched his way to Mamma's side. As she crumpled into his arms, sobbing and begging him for relief from the pain, he took the scissors from her and reached out to hand them to one of us. Ross stepped up and took them from him.

I watched Papà rock Mamma back and forth. He softly murmured, "*Non piangere, Mariamia. Non piangere. Domani. Ti giuro, troviamo un dottore per la testa. Okay?*"

He promised. Tomorrow, he said, he would find a surgeon.

I realized I was silently echoing a part of Papà's repeated plea to Mamma: *Don't cry. Please don't cry.*

And then I realized I was pleading with myself.

Silence

You would think that perhaps we would have called an ambulance or would have driven Mamma to the hospital. You would think that perhaps we would have gotten help, if not for her, then for the rest of us. But you would think wrong.

We simply went to bed.

We were keeping secrets, even when we didn't realize we were keeping secrets. No one outside the family could know, especially when it was doubtful any one of us inside the family really knew.

Cosa nostra.

The next morning, there was no need for Papà to come and wake me. I had barely slept the night before. I could not shake the image of Mamma pressing those scissors into the backside of her head. I wondered what she felt. What was inside her that tormented her so? What evil has such power that it pushes a person to such a point of no return? And if she went down that path, would it really be her fault?

Part of me could not wait to get out of the house and go somewhere—anywhere—besides the house where I found myself to be. Away from what was going on at home. With Mamma. Whatever it was, and whomever else she was talking to.

Sometimes I would catch her, sort of like how Papà would whisper her name to me to tell me something about Mamma in a way that made me suspect he thought others were around to hear whatever he was about to say, and they shouldn't. I'd catch Mamma doing the same, but worse. She wasn't like Papà, who whispered to real people. Mamma said things to nobody, and, worse yet, responded to . . . I'm not sure what or whom. But I was certain there was nobody and nothing around.

She'd sometimes catch me catching her. She'd snap her head around, shaking me, without touching me, to attention. Immediately, I'd look the other way or pretend I wasn't noticing anything about whatever it was she was or wasn't doing. But it'd be too late. She'd follow me around for hours after, wherever I went, from room to room, making direct eye contact, as if trying to pierce me or, at the very least, scare me to death. She succeeded in the latter at times. Her eyes smoldered, not as if they were on fire but more like they were hot, hot coals just doused with cold water. They were the remnants of something no longer there, and yet they threatened with some sort of magical powers, powers she clearly knew she possessed, and they promised pain.

It was becoming clear to me that they were—she was—to be feared and avoided.

I'm not sure if I was the only one in our family to notice it. We never talked about it. Maybe it was just me.

I had once thought that I had magical powers. I now wondered if they were the same as Mamma's.

Back in kindergarten was when I noticed mine. I had a teacher named Ms. Jan: big, blond, and bossy. She wore a hot-pink color on her lips and always seemed to be smiling, even when I could tell that behind her smile, she really wasn't. I think she liked children. I mean, who became a teacher or a *mamma* if they didn't like children? But maybe she liked only the children who did what she wanted them to do. I tried to be that kind of child, but sometimes I just couldn't.

One day, during Art, we all were to put on our smocks and get out our easels and paints and paintbrushes. Ms. Jan said to paint what made us happy. I loved to paint, and I was good at it. "Talented" is what everybody called me. For this masterpiece, I wanted to paint one of those white Easter lilies that have the honey kind of stuff that drips off them and smells so good, you just want to inhale it like you're gonna eat them. Mamma didn't really like flowers all that much, except for violets and this kind of lily that Papà would always buy for her for Easter. Mamma wasn't very good at keeping them alive for very long, so, right after Easter, sometimes before they even died, she'd throw the flowers away. But I'd sneak into the garbage and rescue them, as long as they still smelled sweet, so they could live just a day or two longer.

Easter lilies are pretty much all white. And they have long green stems. Everybody knows that. And nowhere on them is there the color purple. When Ms. Jan came up behind me and looked at my flower, she said, "Oooh, now, isn't that pretty?" But she didn't mean it. I know she didn't, because she took the paintbrush out of my hand and started painting on my flower. With the color purple. She said she could see what I was trying to do and, as she added purple to my no-longer-white lily, kept nodding and saying "Mmmm" to herself. Like she was making it better instead of worse.

"Now, *that's* a beautiful iris," she said, looking at me like I ought to agree or something. I didn't. I didn't even smile back at her phony smile. I wanted to throw all the purple paint all over that picture and Ms. Jan. But I kept my feelings tight inside so no one outside would know. The second she turned around to paint on someone else's drawing, however, I wished her hands would fall off so she wouldn't be able to ruin anyone else's artwork.

I would get my wish.

Ms. Jan disappeared out of sight for a moment. She had taken a number of sheets of colored paper to the little side room in our classroom where the paper cutter was kept. It was sharp and danger-ous, we were told; children weren't allowed in that room without an adult. Maybe Ms. Jan shouldn't have been allowed back there with-out another adult, either.

No one knew what was going on when Ms. Jan screamed and

came running out of that room with a towel wrapped around her hand and blood soaking through the towel and onto the floor. She must have cut her hand off, or at least a couple of fingers.

At that moment, I froze. I watched Ms. Jan try to smile with tears in her eyes and blood all over her hands and smock. All the way out the door of our classroom, she was saying, sort of singsongy, "Everything's okay, kids." She said to stay put and she would have the principal come get us in just a minute. Then she was gone.

But everything was not okay, and I immediately convinced myself that I was responsible. I had wished Ms. Jan's hands would fall off, and they had. I had used what I thought were my magical powers to make that paper cutter cut off her fingers. That's what I thought.

It happened again, sometime during that same year.

My *papà* and I were on our way home from somewhere. I was jumping around in the backseat of our car. And that's when I saw them. Twelve baby ducks. Quacking behind their *mamma*. Right there on the sidewalk.

I screamed, "*Papà, vedi!*" Even though I told him to look, he just couldn't see them. He thought I was imagining the whole thing. But those baby ducks weren't in my imagination. I just knew they were real. And I wanted them. So I wished them to me.

Later that day, Papà was outside when he learned that a neighbor guy had captured the baby ducks and put them in a box. He called for me to come with him to go see them. I knew it. I just knew I wasn't seeing things. I yammered the whole half a block in a joyous "I told you so" song to my *papà*, twirling around with excitement.

But Papà didn't think the way I did. As a matter of fact, when he saw that the babies were in the box all alone, he shook his head and tsk-tsked out a string of "no, no, no, no, no." I didn't understand. I begged my *papà* to let us take them home. The neighbor guy even said okay. This was what I wanted. I knew they were meant to be mine.

"*Per favore, Papà.*" I begged and pleaded until he gave in. We took my babies home. We kept them in the box until Papà could build a little cage of chicken wire for them. Inside we put food and a little plastic swimming pool. We all got to choose names for them: Bonnie, Clyde, Moe, Larry, Curly, Bozo, Cookie, Laurel, Hardy, Abbott, Costello, and Red Skelton. We watched them do backflips into the pool and climb all over one another to eat and sleep all squished together in one mound.

And we watched as their *mamma* flew overhead in endless circles, crying out for her babies. I tried not to think about it.

Until the first little duck died. Then the second one. Then the third.

I begged my *papà* to do something. He moved the cage into the basement of our house and wrapped up the remaining babies in warm towels. But one by one they were dying. I begged my *papà* to let them go back to their *mamma*. "I'm sorry, so sorry," I kept saying, over and over. But Papà said it was too late. He said that once those babies were handled by people, the *mamma* would not touch them again. Because we had taken them, she had no choice but to abandon them. And because they did not have their *mamma*, they could not survive.

What had I done?

I sat on the cold floor in the basement with the last surviving little duck cupped in my hands, trying to keep it warm inside my sweater. I did not know which one he was. Moe? Red? I didn't even know his name.

And I could do nothing more than hold him until he, too, died.

I remember thinking what a horrid *mamma* I had turned out to be.

It was at that point in my young life that I started to realize—real or imagined—my power. And I decided I could not be trusted with it. I wasn't like Glenda the Good Witch. My power leaned more toward the wicked, like the Witch of the West. Whenever I seemed to wish for things, bad things happened.

So, at the age of six, I promised myself I would wish no more; I would stay silent. If I did possess some sort of magic, I would abandon it. I would certainly never wish bad things on anybody, no matter what they did to me. And I would no longer wish for what I wanted, because when I got it, somehow, whatever it was I'd gotten ended up being twisted and not at all what I had dreamed it would be.

It was a promise I tried to keep, but, inevitably, I kept breaking it. And every time I broke that promise, bad things would happen. I would be to blame. I would be reminded of what a bad girl I really was. And it would reinforce in me the thought that I deserved whatever bad came my way.

So, while one part of me could not sleep because I couldn't stop thinking about Mamma and wanted to get away from whatever had a hold on her, even if just for one more day, another part of me could not sleep because I could not stop myself from wishing that when I got to work at the donut shop, I'd get to see Gunner again.

I knew it was dangerous to wish it. I could sense how wrong it felt. But I just couldn't help myself.

Would he remember the night before and say something to me? Or would he act as if nothing had happened? Did Officer Brown pick him up after Papà and I left for home? How long did he have to wait? Did he tell Officer Brown what we talked about? What happened to the man with the hospital bracelet?

In my head, I practiced different presentations of each. First I asked a question as if I were super excited to hear the answer. Then I asked the same question as if I couldn't have cared less and was just being a polite server. I would choose which ones to deliver when I assessed the situation, I decided.

I made mental notes of all the questions I would ask if my wish came true and he showed up—but it was more than that. I didn't just wish for him to show; I wished that he would show up *and* acknowledge me, not just as the donut girl behind the counter but as the "very adult" person he said I was, who had impressed him with how I'd handled myself. I wanted Gunner to say something or do something that let everyone else know I mattered and possessed the magic powers for good.

Black. Two sugars. Strawberry-iced raised donut. I would also make sure, the second I saw his squad car pull up, to have his order at the ready.

My thoughts focused back on the present as I heard Papà thumping his way down the stairs to where I was, just as the kitchen clock struggled to tick its big hand onto the number 12. For some reason, one Papà couldn't figure out, something always made it stick for just a few seconds every hour on the hour. It didn't bother him enough to fix it. And it didn't bother me, because every time I heard that loud *click*, I knew another hour had just passed me by. Plus, because of the little bit of time we lost with every extra second the hand took to round the dial, I could fool myself into thinking I always had just a little bit more time for whatever it was I needed.

It was 6:00 a.m. The coffee I had started was just snorting out its last drops. I had to be at the donut shop by 7:00 a.m., and Papà needed to drive me.

I poured myself a cup. I sat in one of the vinyl chairs at our white Formica table with little gold scrolls that circled its oval shape. The cushion under my seat whispered an exhalation. I looked up at the off-white walls, wondering if they had originally been white and now were just a dirty shadow of their former selves, or if, indeed, we had painted them that color. If you could call it a color. The entire kitchen—the entire house, actually—was void of it.

I wondered, too, about what Papà had said to Mamma. About finding her a surgeon who would crack her skull open, take a look around, and stop her pain. I wondered how he was going to do what he'd promised he would do. Maybe he knew something more than I did. But I doubted it; I had become Papà's translator, letter writer, phone-call maker, insurance negotiator—pretty much his consigliere, just like in the *Godfather* movie. I was his right-hand girl. His advisor. If Papà did have a surgeon on the line, I'd know about it.

But what if I didn't? What if Papà did have a surgeon at the ready and my hands had never been involved in making it happen? I wondered, how would he have found this surgeon all on his own? And why wouldn't he have looped me in from the start?

What if he didn't need me any longer? Who was I going to be then?

"*Che pensi, Paolamia*?" Papà kissed me on the top of my head, nonchalantly asking me what I was thinking, while on his way to pouring himself a cup of my coffee.

I thought about it. His question. My possible answers. I thought about point-blank asking him about Mamma and this—what I was sure was a phantom—surgeon promise. I thought about asking him if there was something more wrong with Mamma, something that maybe even a scalpel wouldn't fix. I thought about asking him what he thought about the guy he'd met at the donut shop the night before—my cop friend.

And then I thought better of it.

"*Niente*, Papà."

Sabotage

I shielded my eyes from the sun's glare as it seemed to teeter on the very corner of the donut shop's rooftop. Its early-morning brilliance splashed across the parking lot's blacktop, ricocheting off any surrounding metal and chrome and whitewashing the all-glass front windows and door to the point where both Papà and I had to search for the handle to pull, as if we were two blind folks missing our canes.

Hearing the tinkle of the angel bells let me know Papà had finally found the way in, and we crossed the threshold into the still-silent shop. The sweet scents of fried dough and chocolate and frostings of maple and strawberry caressed my senses, and I felt welcomed home. Through the interior window on the left, the one that gave a partial view into the back room, I could see the two donut bakers—each one a carbon copy of Mr. Kumar—finishing up their work, quickly shifting fresh-baked treats from ovens and fryers to rows upon rows of drying racks.

I did not see Karen or Aurora or even Mr. Kumar yet, but I was early for the start of my 7:00 a.m. shift. My regular Saturday hours of 3:00 p.m. to 11:30 p.m. wouldn't start until next week, after one more weekend of training. Today, I would learn how to frost and fill!

I so wanted to get started *now*.

"*Ciao, Papà.*" I hurriedly kissed him good-bye, hoping to send him on his way before anyone else saw that a parent was dropping me off. How babyish, and just not cool, I thought, for somebody who was supposed to be already sixteen and of driving age.

"*Ci vediamo alle tre*," Papà said. He seemed in an equal hurry to leave me, saying nothing more than that he'd see me again when he picked me up at 3:00 p.m. I was a bit surprised he was so eager to go. It wasn't like him, at least not with me.

As I watched him turn to leave, I made sure to confirm: "*Si, ci vediamo alle tre, Papà.*"

I let out a tiny sigh of relief when, as he walked out the door, he called over his shoulder in his best English, "Have good day, baby girl."

Whatever it was inside me that was feeling whatever it was that I was feeling relaxed.

Mr. Kumar and Aurora emerged from the back room.

"You punch in?" Mr. Kumar asked, with a jerk of his head directed at me.

I shook my head.

He gestured for me to do so.

As I crossed in front of them both to make my way to the punch clock, Aurora began slowly shaking her head. Disapproval.

"Dahlink, what's this?" She pointed to my apron, stained with sugars, drips, and drizzles of donut remnants from the day before. I had had no time to wash my uniform the night before, nor had I really even thought about it. I was instantly ashamed.

"Dirty girl," Aurora scolded, but with a smirk and a wink that made me smile, just a little bit, back. "Come on." She took my hand and started leading me through the baking area to the back-office area. "We'll get you a fresh one."

Mr. Kumar stopped us, his hands waving in the air as if he were in some Jazzercise class.

"No, no, no. She'll stay dirty today," he snorted to Aurora. "In the back, here." Then he looked at me. "Today, you learn to make the donuts."

That's exactly what I wished for, I thought, trying to contain my excitement.

At that moment, Karen whooshed in, looking a bit disheveled and yammering about something and something-something that had made her later than she should have been. No apology, though.

Mr. Kumar sort of waved us all away, turned, and disappeared into his back, back office.

The angel bells tinkled, ushering in the morning's first customers. Karen and Aurora took over the front while I remained with the bakers in the back.

From where I was positioned, I could not see the ladies working the counter. My only view out was through that little side window, and I could barely see much more than a sliver of the customers coming in, and then only if they stood directly in front of the cash register and that first lowboy display, the one where we kept the specialty donuts, like apple fritters or giant cinnamon rolls, the new muffins, or those new, filled donut holes.

I thought it was ingenious how those little balls of dough even came to be: the holes from the centers of the big donuts—holes that used to be discarded or mushed back together with more dough to make other big donuts. I thought about how they weren't thought to be important enough on their own. Leftover dough. Throwaways. I wondered who had been the first person to see them for something more than what they were considered to be. I wondered who had been the first to figure out that these holes were whole and good enough all on their own. I wondered.

Next to my buttermilk balls and French crullers, these specialty donut holes were my favorites. I loved them. Even loved what they were called: munchkins. I loved saying the word. "M-u-n-c-h-k-i-n-s." Like those little people in *The Wizard of Oz*: fully adult but still the size of small kids. And now these donut holes had something even newer happening with them. They now came filled with custard and chocolate cream and different jellies. I thought it funny that I would be able to say I was filling up a hole, literally, when the whole thing in and of itself was a hole. Or at least called a hole. *And* I was super excited that I would get to do the honors—at least I hoped I would—sometime today.

I made a promise to myself that the first chance I got, I would double-fill a still-warm powdered-sugar donut hole with strawberry jelly and pop it into my mouth—hopefully without getting caught. You really weren't supposed to be eating the merchandise. That's what Mr. Kumar said. But I noticed Karen had done it a lot the week before. She'd just made sure nobody was looking; then she'd gobbled down a few.

We started on my little sister Viny's favorites: round, raised donuts that we would frost with white icing and half dip in multicolored sprinkles. Of course, the bakers didn't know they were her favorites, just as I really didn't know any of the bakers. They didn't even introduce themselves. No names. They just set me up at my station—a smoothly polished length of stainless-steel counter—wheeled a few racks of naked donuts to one side of me and the vats of frostings and sprinkly stuff to the other, then connected a yellow plastic hourglass contraption to the plug in the wall over by the corner, saying to me one word—"jelly"—and that was pretty much it. Mr. Kumar was the one who then stepped in to give me a hands-on lesson in the fine art of frosting and filling.

Only it wasn't as fine as I had imagined in my head.

Mr. Kumar kept coughing up phlegm and snorting and swallowing it. Sometimes, I swear, he even seemed to sneeze right into his hand and still kept touching the donuts. Without washing in between. I started out mentally marking the donuts I thought he had infected, planning on tossing them out the moment his back was turned, but there were so many, and they all looked so alike, that I lost track. So I just tried to ignore it, promising myself I would make sure that whatever donuts I ate or took home were ones I had touched, free from anyone else's filth.

Mr. Kumar's teaching method didn't involve many words. His favorite seemed to be "watch."

So I did.

He took a donut in one hand, literally gave it a smackdown into the vat of frosting, then lifted it and placed it on a different tray to dry, one already set with pink paper so that it would be ready when it needed to be placed out front.

That was it. Lesson one was over.

Piece of cake, I thought.

When it was my turn, I took one of the donuts, slam-dunked it into the vat of white icing, then reached in to grab and lift it out . . . but it tore apart. I tried to pluck it out, but it wasn't coming. Or, to be more accurate, it was coming out, but in pieces.

Mr. Kumar shook his head and sort of laughed, but it was more like a sneer. Like he knew something that I was too stupid to comprehend.

"Watch!" he commanded.

So I did. Again.

Mr. Kumar repeated all the steps, but this time I realized what I'd done wrong. I had tried to pull that donut out of its swimming pool of gooey, sticky goodness straight up. What Mr. Kumar did was coax it, sort of caressing it and turning it clockwise, as he slid it up and out.

I was impressed. And ready to try again. And this time, I produced a beautifully frosted specimen, complete with a bit of a curly wisp that settled onto the top and gave it a bit of flair.

At least I thought so.

Mr. Kumar just nodded and snorted and said, "You do three each kind, then three, then three . . ." I turned to where he was pointing. But he was pointing all over the place. Toward dozens of donuts on dozens of rows on dozens of racks. All waiting for me to finish them.

As excited as I was, I couldn't ignore that little voice in me that kept pointing out that this all seemed like a lot of work. Especially for just one me. The donut bakers were already putting on their jackets, preparing to go home. I would be solo in this frost-and-fill venture. And suddenly I wasn't sure this was going to be as much fun as I had thought it would be. That little voice even warned I would get a hand cramp. I told it to shut up, and I focused on double-filling and maybe even creatively frosting a bunch of treats that I would then take home with me. I could imagine Mamma's face lighting up as she bit into a double-stuffed, cream-filled, chocolate-covered donut hole. I'd even add sprinkles to it. She'd just have to pop it into her mouth. One tiny bite, an explosion of flavors in her mouth, requiring the tiniest of efforts. Even she could do it and enjoy it, no matter how tired she was or how much pain she was in.

And *that* would make *this* all worth it.

By the time I turned back around, Mr. Kumar had moved on to the marble effect. He wasn't even waiting for me. It almost seemed like he didn't really care whether or not I was watching; he certainly didn't seem to care if I was actually learning.

I saw him take his entire hand, dip the tips of his five fingers into a vat of chocolate icing, and then let it drip down over a batch of white-iced donuts lying on a pink paper–lined silver tray. The result was an artistic harmony of black-and-white swirls that gave the marble donut its name.

There was no time for me to practice the move, however, as Mr. Kumar continued to move hurriedly down the assembly line; he was already working on the contraption that oozed out jellies and creams.

Again, he turned to me: "Watch!"

I nodded.

He reached into a rack and pulled out two undressed donuts. Not the kind of donuts with a hole in the middle, though—these candidates were round and puffy and missing any hole. They were so fat, it was obvious they were born to be filled.

With one hand, he took one of the donuts, plopped it into the vat of chocolate frosting, and swirled it out, just as he had done with those other donuts in lesson one. He kept that donut in one hand while with his other hand he grabbed the other donut, tossed it into a vat of sugar, and then fished it out. Then, with a donut in each hand, he pushed one onto the milky-white plastic nozzle that protruded from the bottom right of the contraption and pushed the other onto the identical-looking tube to the left. With his fists, he quickly depressed the metal bar directly underneath the donuts and the machine started to hum. It pushed out the exact right amount of custard (that went into the chocolate-covered donut) and strawberry jelly (that went into the sugared donut).

It all happened in seconds. And I couldn't help but be amazed, not only at the entire process, but also at how acrobatic it looked in Mr. Kumar's hands. At that moment, I even dismissed how dirty those hands might be.

The look of awe must have shown on my face, because when Mr. Kumar looked at me to ask, simply, "Okay?" he seemed to startle just a bit, and I swear he blushed and shrugged. And then he left me.

"More tomorrow," he said as he walked away, into the back room. A flick of his hand over his head brought with it another command: "You do now."

His reaction made me wonder if he was the way he seemed to be because nobody ever made him feel like what he did was special. I wondered. Maybe, like those donut holes, Mr. Kumar needed somebody to make him feel like he mattered and was worthy on his own.

Maybe.

I turned to face the racks of donuts awaiting my attention, and my eyes caught sight of Gunner, standing at the register. I couldn't see much of him through the window. I doubted he could see me at all. I watched as he took a large coffee to go. He raised it to his lips and took a big gulp. How he didn't burn himself, I just didn't know. I tried to make motions to get his attention, without motioning so much that anybody would think I was trying to get his attention. But he, too, seemed in a hurry, and before I even got a chance to get myself out to the front room, he turned and walked out. He must not have seen me.

For the remainder of that day, I sulked.

Karen and Aurora popped in every now and again to quickly

ask, "You doin' okay?" or to shout out some order that needed filling: "We're out of double chocolates, girl. Get some out here, please."

But for the most part, in that back room, I felt as if I were in solitary confinement. Surrounded by temptations that I really couldn't eat. Kept behind a glass and a wall, away from people I really couldn't reach. Talking to myself or, as usual, singing along with whatever tune was playing on the radio. Thank God for the radio. Not only did it help drown out the laughter and fun of what was going on in the front room without me, but it also seemed to speak to me, answer whatever thoughts were in my head. I don't know exactly when I noticed it, but every lyric seemed to be some message meant for me. I wanted to believe it was God speaking to me. But sometimes—like when Rod Stewart asked questions about being sexy and wanting somebody's body—I knew those lyrics were coming from someone else. No way would God talk like that. Would He?

The hours crawled.

Not even double-filling that powdered-sugar donut hole and sneaking it into my mouth gave me the pleasure I thought it would. My hands did get crampy. And my feet and back were *killing* me.

I couldn't wait until Papà showed up.

Only I would wait. And wait.

I waited on the little pink stool out at the front of the shop. By myself. Long after Karen and Aurora left for home. Mr. Kumar was taking over the afternoon shift. Starting next week, he would no longer have to. I would. But at that moment, I was debating again whether or not I really wanted to come back. And the longer I waited, the more my answer was no.

More than thirty minutes after my quitting time, I finally saw Papà's white Catalina come barreling into the parking lot, the headlights flashing three times.

"*Totally unnecessary,*" I squeaked to myself in disgust, trying to keep unexpected tears at bay. *"And you're late. And I've been look-ing out for you for the longest time. I don't need flashing headlights; I needed you here when you promised you'd be here!"*

I didn't quite know why I felt so angry. I knew only that I did. Maybe because he had forgotten me. Maybe because Gunner hadn't even looked for me, probably didn't even miss me. Maybe because what I had wished for now made me feel like *The Wizard of Oz*'s Tin Man, needing some oil in my back and on my knees and my hand.

When Papà entered the donut shop, looking all goofy and giddy for some reason, I was ready for him. Ready to shoot off my mouth.

Until he said what he said.

"Paolamia, la mamma avrà la sua operazione sulla testa prima di Natale!"

What did I just hear him say? I couldn't believe it. He had done it. Mamma was going to get her head operation before Christmas. He had kept his promise. To her.

I didn't think. I barely paused. Again, the look on my face must have communicated what I was thinking, because Papà's joy melted away from his. I had just opened my mouth, about to shed my tears and scream at him, something like, "What about me?" when the angel bells tinkled.

"Well, hello, *POWwww*leeena and *POWwww*leeena's father! Mr. Tony!"

Gunner stepped in.

Instantly, my tears dried up, as did any thought of spewing any kind of wrath upon my *papà*. I had to consciously tell myself to close my mouth and just smile.

Papà extended his hand.

Gunner shook it. "You dropping our girl off?"

I blurted out, "Oh, no, I already worked my shift this morning. My father's just picking me up."

Gunner's eyebrows raised, as if surprised. "I didn't see you here this morning."

My heart and my thoughts started to race. *He* did *look for me when he came in earlier. Maybe he left so quickly because he figured I wasn't here. Was he here now for the same reason . . . to see me?*

Papà understood enough of the conversation to join in: "Mr. Tim. I come little late. My baby girl, she be wait for me."

Then he directed an apology to me and joked, as he often did with me, that he was a "bad father": "*Scuzami, Paoletta. Papà è monello.*"

I felt so wrong. Wrong in my anger toward Papà. Wrong in my thoughts about Gunner. Whatever I seemed to be thinking, I felt wrong in thinking it.

"It's okay, Papà. *Non è niente.*"

"Now, *POWwww*leeeena, you're going to have to really start teaching me that Italian if you're gonna talk about me." Gunner winked and smiled, showing off his perfect teeth.

I couldn't think straight. I needed to just stop thinking. And for everybody around me to stop talking. I stammered, "I just said it was nothing. That's all. I didn't say anything about you. Um. But we have to get going. My mom . . ."

Oh my God, what was I doing? What was I going to say? I needed us to go now, before my thoughts and my mouth could do any real damage.

"*Papà, andiamo.*"

Papà nodded and, with one hand, made a sweeping "after you" motion to me. He then extended that hand again to Gunner. "We see again."

Gunner nodded, still smiling. Just as I opened the door, underscored by the angel bells, he called out, "So what *are* your hours, *POWwww*leeeena?"

I turned, praying that my face didn't look as red as it felt. It took a moment to find my voice. I swallowed. And gave him what he wanted.

Suspicion

They would be making a hole, maybe two, in Mamma's skull. It would happen soon. By December, for sure way before Christmas, this "exploratory surgery" was a guarantee to fix whatever was wrong with Mamma's head and to stop her pain and suffering. By then I would already be halfway through the eighth grade, I thought to myself as Papà continued, talking with his hands more than was usual even for him. He had become so animated with his gestures that I was nervously watching him and his hands *not* on the wheel, rather than wholeheartedly listening to what he was saying during our entire car ride home.

I didn't understand how it could be possible. Not just the part about how Papà had been able to get this done, all on his own, but the part about how a bunch of doctors thought it a good idea to just go poking around the inside of somebody's brain to "explore" without really knowing what it was they were looking for.

Papà said that his good friend Dr. Joseph Scarmazzo had gotten us in.

Dr. Scarmazzo? I thought to myself. *Can't be.* I knew only one Dr. Scarmazzo. He was Ross's godfather. And if it was the same guy, then that Dr. Scarmazzo was an obstetrician. He did his best work on the lower end of the female body. What did he know about what was right when it came to Mamma's head?

Dr. Scarmazzo had delivered Ross and, as my *papà* recounted whenever talking about the blessed birth of his only son, had started screaming in the halls of the hospital room, all the way to where my *papà* was waiting, calling out, "*Antonino . . . è nato Rosario Milana!*"

Every time I heard that story and envisioned Dr. Scarmazzo shouting my *papà*'s name and announcing that a boy had been born, meaning—as any good Sicilian would know—that the paternal grandfather would now have a namesake, it made me think of the baby Jesus and the angels trumpeting His arrival. And ever since both births, it had been clear to family and friends that kings were indeed born. One ended up being the Savior, the other my brother.

Now, as some sort of early Christmas present, just before the former's birthday, another miracle would happen, and my *mamma* would be cured.

Something inside me just didn't buy it. I wanted to. I wanted to wish that this would make everything better, but I was afraid to, given my wishing track record. And I didn't want to tell my *papà* what I was really thinking about it, because I already had squashed his enthusiasm once today. I didn't want to hurt him again. So I said nothing, only nodding as if in agreement, knowing that he needed me to believe. And so I pretended to.

I wondered what Mamma was feeling. Was she scared? Nervous? Did she believe that this would make everything better?

The moment I entered the front door of our home, I would know.

She pulled me into the foyer and wrapped her arms around me in an intensely fierce embrace. I squeezed my eyes shut, immediately thinking I had done something wrong, bracing for a blow. But then I heard laughter. And it was coming from her. And kisses. Planted on me.My first thought was that I regretted not having brought home any of her favorite donuts to help make whatever this celebration was even sweeter. My second thought was to make a wish that this scheduled miracle would make everything better.

I allowed myself to melt into Mamma's arms. I looked up at her smiling face. God, she was so beautiful. Her skin was flawless, a milky, poreless porcelain. She was even wearing her signature blood-red lipstick. I couldn't remember the last time I had seen it on her.

She released me, and I looked at the faces of each member of my family, now assembled together and walking together into our kitchen to sit down and eat a meal together.

Together.

I don't remember what we ate. I just remember everyone talking, almost at the same time. Even my sisters, Cathy and Viny. About happy things. About the future. About what we were going to do when Mamma was finally fixed.

It felt, in a way, like a dream. Fuzzy around the edges. Colors that seemed to come alive. Voices that echoed, sometimes as if from a record player on a speed too slow for me to really understand the words being said.

It was my sister Cathy who broke through my fog, asking if I wanted a ride to the party.

I had no idea what she was talking about.

I had forgotten that St. Peter had one of its roller-skating parties that night. It was weird for Cathy to offer to drive me, though. And I decided that the dream couldn't be real. As a matter of fact, it was slowly starting to feel like a setup. Cathy never volunteered to do anything, unless something was in it for her.

I tested out my theory.

"So, were you wanting to go to the party, too?"

"Don't be an idiot. Why would I want to go to some grade-school roller-skating party? I was just being nice. But forget it."

That was more what I was used to.

I hadn't planned on going to the party. I hadn't even remembered that tonight was the night St. Peter had scheduled it. It wasn't like I couldn't go. I wasn't working. And this might be the last Saturday night I could even say that. I had a ride there and a ride back. Both Mamma and Papà had heard what Cathy said, and they weren't saying I couldn't go. They weren't saying anything. They just kept smiling. So I could leave everyone, just for the night, and not worry about anyone or anything, other than me, for a change.

I agreed and took Cathy up on her offer.

"Well, hurry up, then—get washed and change," she said. "I'm not driving you so smelly and dirty, like you are in that uniform."

I looked down at myself. I hadn't realized it, but she was right. If I'd been dirty that morning when Aurora had first seen me, a whole day of frosting and filling had made me positively gross.

Yet my *mamma* had hugged me anyway.

I raced up the stairs to my bedroom. I looked in my closet. One of the ladies Mamma had sewn dresses for had given her a top, too little for Mamma but perfect for me. I touched it. It felt so smooth and cool. It shimmered, even. It was red, the most beautiful red I had ever seen. It even had this big bow that tied at the very top. I imagined myself wearing it, looking like a beautifully wrapped Christmas present.

I so wanted to wear it, but Mamma didn't think red was a color I should be wearing. She said only bad girls wore red. I didn't dare ask why Mamma wore nearly the very same color red on her lips. But I thought about it. And I tried not to wonder why Mamma would even have given me the top in the first place, if she wasn't even going to let me wear it, but I did worry. I left the top and chose something else.

"Let's goooo . . . !" Cathy bellowed from the bottom of the stairs.

I grabbed jeans and some other top and clean underwear and raced into the bathroom to shower.

"Five minutes!" I yelled back at her, knowing I'd be at least ten or fifteen. She must have someplace else to be, and I, just a stop along the way, was now making her late.

I dried myself off, blow-dried my hair, dressed myself, picked up my dirty clothes, and opened the bathroom door.

Mamma was standing there.

I let out a little yelp. Normally, her being there would have been, well, normal. I would have been prepared for it. But I wasn't thinking, and for a second I had let my guard down.

She held out her hands and asked for my dirty uniform and other discarded things.

"*Paoletta, dammi che li posso lavare per domani.*"

She was volunteering to wash my clothes so I'd be clean for tomorrow.

I handed them over to her. I noticed she was smiling. And it looked real.

"*Grazie, Mamma.*" I didn't know what else to say.

I thought about going back into my bedroom closet, pulling out that red top, and wearing it. But I didn't want to tempt fate or ruin whatever magic was at play and helping to make Mamma more normal. For however long it would last, I would take it and try not to do anything to mess it up.

Cathy dropped me off in front of the rink. It was called the Playdium. The place was all concrete on the outside, lit up with lights that made it look like white icing that had hardened. The building was even shaped like a round donut, like one of those puffy ones without a hole but with filling in the center.

I could hear the pounding music from where I stood in the parking lot. Cathy had already driven off, not having bothered to make sure I would get inside. But I didn't care. For one night, I was free, and I was about to enter a place filled with school friends and songs I loved to sing and roller skates that were like soft leather boots, not like the all-metal roller skates I had at home that attached, barely, to your regular shoes. And nobody to tell me that whatever I chose to think or say or do was anything other than okay.

No sooner had I said my hellos to my girlfriends from school and finished lacing up my skates than the DJ started to play one of my favorites, the Bee Gees' "If I Can't Have You."

I loved *Saturday Night Fever*. And this was my favorite song from it. I knew every word. I sang along in my head.

"You wanna skate?"

I lifted my head and nearly toppled over. Danny—*Danny*—was asking me if I wanted to skate.

"With you?"

I immediately wanted to die. What a stupid question. Why couldn't my mouth wait until I gave it the okay to speak?

Danny just smiled, half laughing. His tousled brown hair swung a bit as he gave me his hand. I took it. And we skated. To Yvonne Elliman. Round and round, the lights—blue and red and green— all flashing around us. I felt almost dizzy. I felt as if I was not just dreaming but *was* the dream. Wherever I looked, faces and other skaters blurred. I could barely even attempt to look at Danny, but I did. I got up the courage to do it, to focus on his face, and couldn't believe that he was looking back at me, smiling. I had to look away. My face, I knew, was getting red. I could feel it. My hair was starting to stick to me, too.

I tried to pay attention to the words of the song. I tried to make myself calm down and cool off. But when I listened to the words, more questions came to mind. What were they trying to tell me? What was the message in the lyrics? Had Danny picked this exact song to skate to with me? Was he trying to tell me that he had to have me?

Danny was in the grade ahead of me. His little brother Jimmy was in my same grade, but I didn't think of Jimmy in any way other than as another boy in my class. A smart boy. A nice boy. But just another boy. Danny was like Ricky. Ricky was another boy in my same grade, but he looked and acted like he belonged in high school already. He was tall and thin and had spiky blond hair. He wore shirts with the sleeves cut off so his biceps showed. He would have fit perfectly as one of John Travolta's boys in *Grease*. He even smoked cigarettes and drank. And he had a reputation. For being bad. Danny was just like Ricky, sort of. Not in how he looked. And Danny didn't smoke or drink. Or if he did, he hadn't yet gotten a bad reputation because of it or anything else. Danny was like Ricky in the way he made the girls feel. But Danny seemed safe. Or safer. At least to me.

I started to breathe more heavily than what I thought was normal. I couldn't seem to catch my breath, but I didn't want the song to end, the skating to end.

When the song was over, Danny escorted me back to where he had picked me up. He said thanks and then skated off. All the girls around me started chattering, asking me what it was like, skating with Danny. It was a big deal. He didn't skate with just anybody.

I shrugged my shoulders and tossed back my head, not sure of how to answer. If I said it was the most incredible feeling, would that be too much? If I said it was great, would that be enough? If I said it was okay, would they think me stuck up? I settled on saying one word: "Wow!" Over and over, that was all I would say. And, based on their reactions, it was the perfect response.

As the air became cooler, the trees began bursting with color. Maples were my favorite. Reds, oranges, yellows. As much as I loved seeing those autumn leaves, I knew that their brilliance was short-lived. They were destined to dry out, die off, and drop to the ground, exposing their unprotected limbs.

I wondered if they knew what they were headed for.

In a way, I was feeling just like those maple trees: on the verge of exploding, wanting to, ready to show off my own colors but deathly afraid of what that might lead to. I felt as if I were charting the unknown, with no one around to help me figure out what to do. As excited as I was, I felt much more comfortable in what I had been living, what I already knew.

To complicate matters even more, I felt as if everything I already knew and had become accustomed to navigating, even controlling, was starting to change, too.

Mamma seemed happier than I had seen her in I didn't know how long. Papà was always humming of late, focused on getting everything ready for the upcoming surgery. I was making great tips at the donut shop and had already surpassed both Karen and Aurora in terms of my Sunday-morning popularity with the regulars. Or at least I thought I had. Gunner had started coming in on both Friday nights and Saturday nights to sit with me and talk with me, and when Papà couldn't make it to come get me, Gunner would even drive me home.

And I was handling it all like a grown-up.

But something was feeling funny or a bit off to me. Inside, I was more unsettled than ever before.

When I thought about it, I realized that for me, school was what I had always been able to count on. It was a no-brainer: same thing, day after day. Stable. Everything outside of school, however, was usually pretty unstable. I had grown used to that. So, in a way, that instability had become my stability.

But now it seemed as if everything outside of what I used to count on or think of as a no-brainer—everything other than school, that is—was now sort of going okay. Better than I could have wished for. It was as if some giant black hole had opened up, some parallel universe, and Mamma and the family and the donut shop and even Gunner seemed all under control. Normal, even. While I suppose I should have been happy about it and looked at it as a good thing, my instability's becoming stability made me feel more unstable. I didn't trust it. I just couldn't help but feel that the minute I let my guard down, the minute I fully relaxed and believed, *that* would be the very moment when the other shoe would drop and I, like those maple trees in winter, would be exposed, unprotected.

It scared me because inside me, I could feel myself letting go, wanting to.

At the same time, the one place where I always felt pretty much in control—school—seemed to be spiraling downward, becoming very much out of control for me. And that unnerved me, too. The very thing that gave me stability was starting to shake beneath me. And I couldn't put my finger on my feelings, on why I felt the way I did.

It was sort of like that movie *Freaky Friday*, where one day Jodie Foster's character wakes up, realizes she's switched lives with her own mother, and is forced to learn how to navigate adulthood while making sure her mom doesn't screw up her childhood. That was how I felt: as if people and places and situations had suddenly swapped places. And as much as I thought I might be ready to emerge as something or someone new and take on someone or something new, to shine for however long my colorful brilliance lasted, I was afraid and felt much more comfortable staying in my off-white, subdued shell, knowing what to expect, where to expect it, and from whom. Even if what I knew to expect was never to expect the expected.

Something was for sure happening at school. Something definitely unexpected. But before I knew what it was, it was too late; it had already happened.

For weeks, we were to have been practicing our dance routines. The music teacher, Mrs. Lavergne, had given everyone in class, the girls *and* the boys, an assignment to get into teams of no more than three and to do some sort of dance routine to a piece of music of our choice.

Mrs. Lavergne was nice enough but sort of stuck in her own adolescent years. She had Mary Tyler Moore hair; she even wore it the same way the actress did on the show that bore her name. And she had saucer-size brown eyes that always seemed on the verge of tears. A couple of times, our class had actually made her cry. I don't remember why, exactly, but I do remember Mr. Jaminez, our eighth-grade homeroom teacher—part priest reject and part military sergeant—warning us not to do it again.

This dance-routine thing could have been something we wanted to make her cry about. But the threat of Mr. Jaminez ensured we didn't.

I don't know why Mrs. Lavergne was having us do it. It seemed odd to me then, still does now. The most we ever really did in Music Appreciation was appreciate music, listen to it—not ever dance to it. We barely really sang anything, and never the modern stuff. So I had no clue why she was having us do these dance routines. Nobody knew.

What I did know was that my friends Gaby and Lily and Jackie had secretly formed their own group and left me to find my own.

That was an example of one of the things making me feel "off" at school.

I was more of a friend to Gaby and Lily than Jackie had ever been. Why would they have picked her and not me? I felt discarded, no longer "in." I didn't show it, but I was hurt. I also wasn't asked to join any of the other groups I would have thought I already belonged to. I don't remember whom I ended up having to team up with, but I do remember that they were some girls who weren't really in my group, or at least I didn't consider them to be. Don't get me wrong—it wasn't like I was in the "cool girls" club with people like Meghan or Rachel. Those girls were out of my league. Redheaded, daredevil Meghan and blond-haired, blue-eyed, big-boobed Rachel were looked up to by the girls and lusted after by the boys. I wasn't a member of that club; I really didn't consider myself a member of any club or clique. But for the first time, I felt myself a nonmember, an outsider, someone not good enough for *anyone* to want to be friends with. And I didn't know why. What had I done?

On the day that Gaby and Lily and Jackie were to perform, they must have been feeling guilty or something, because they asked me to fill a hole for them: they needed someone to start and stop the music. They couldn't think of anybody they wanted more than me to be that somebody.

I said yes.

We had all gathered in Mrs. Lavergne's music room—not much

more than a room with a piano in it and a bunch of desks and chairs. We moved everything deemed unnecessary for the performance to the outer rims of the room. I sat in the corner behind all three girls, facing the class, and pushed PLAY on the tape recorder, cranking up Billy Joel's "Only the Good Die Young."

I think everybody was a little surprised at the choice of music. I know I was. I mean, it wasn't exactly a Catholic school–appropriate tune. And yet I listened to those lyrics and thought once again that maybe I was meant to play DJ because I was meant to get this message. What I couldn't figure out, however, was what that message really was. What was God really telling me to do? Was it even God? I felt so sure about these songs speaking to me . . .

That reminded me. We had already been confirmed, the year before, in the seventh grade, just after I'd had my thirteenth birthday. We'd sort of doubled up on the parties. I was pretty sure I'd missed out on the gifts I could have gotten if our confirmation date had been at any other time during the year.

I was already supposed to be in a "state of grace," or so said Father Murgoff in church. But nobody said what that really was or what to do if you thought you weren't. Or maybe I'd missed that part.

We had to choose a new confirmation name. Whichever saint we chose, we had to write a paper on him or her. I had so wished that Dahlia were the name of some saint somewhere. But it wasn't. At least not one that I could find. So I settled on Anne, in honor of the Virgin Mary's mother. My *mamma* liked my choice of names, mostly because I had chosen the name of a saint who had gotten credit for being somebody's *mamma*. But I could tell she was hurt at my choice of sponsor.

Confirmation sponsors were like a spare pair of godparents. I chose a lady named Vita; her name meant "life" in Italian, and she was so alive. Always smiling and laughing and talking, excited about everything. She was the same age as Mamma and married to Mr. Sam Villardita, who'd grown up with Mamma in the same little town in Sicily. Mrs. Villardita had three children of her own, all boys.

She had desperately wanted a daughter but had never ended up actually having one. When she met me, she couldn't stop talking about how pretty I was, and funny and smart, and how much she wished I was her girl.

I ignored those looks that Mamma was giving me—the same ones she gave me when I would sit with Papà, my arm looped through his, on the couch while watching TV. I had to stop myself from unlooping my arm and sitting somewhere else. I thought that if I did that, I would be confirming whatever Mamma was thinking. Admitting guilt for something I didn't do. With Mrs. Villardita, I knew it was wrong to let her go on and on about me, but I loved just basking in her praise. It felt so good, I couldn't stop smiling. She kept hugging me, too, and asking me all sorts of questions about school and boys, wanting to know everything about me. Acting as if whatever I said mattered. In her eyes, I could see that not only was I normal, I was perfect. And she wanted me.

As much as I felt myself drifting, disconnected from all the jumping and twirling and bopping that was taking place in front of me, I really wasn't aware of it. I had become lost in lyrics and in my own thoughts. As usual. Until I heard the next few lines about Catholic girls starting much too late . . .

I shocked myself to attention and spastically pushed the STOP button on the tape recorder. Only one problem: the girls weren't done with their routine; the song wasn't even over. I had stopped it way too early. And all three of my friends turned and hissed at me with screams of "How could you?" and "It's not over!" and "You ruined it!" while the rest of the class clapped, laughed, and cheered.

I wanted to crawl away and die.

I knew it was an honest accident. I hadn't meant to ruin their routine. Or at least I didn't think I had. I wasn't really sure.

The truth didn't matter anyway. It wouldn't have stopped the rest of the class from coming to their own conclusions.

On that same day, as my classmates whispered in the halls—of what, I did not know for sure, but had a feeling it had something to do with me—I would learn that what I had thought was normal, okay, safe behavior at the roller-skating party had somehow turned into rumors of things I had allegedly done. With the boys.

All of which was untrue.

But just like my *mamma* and the things that she thought about me that weren't true, now even my classmates were coming to the same conclusions. And I didn't know why.

I wondered how the swirling conversations about me had even started. And then I wondered if it was all in my head. Maybe they weren't talking about me. Maybe they were treating me the way they always did, only now I was actually noticing. Maybe the voices I heard were all in my head. Like Mamma.

I was scaring myself. Unsure of so many things. So many thoughts. When I was right. When I was wrong. What was good. What was bad. What was my fault. What wasn't. What was normal. What was anything but. Whom could I trust? Could I even trust myself?

Seduction

How he managed to get in, I couldn't begin to guess. But there he was. Night after night. Behind the milk-glass sign that displayed donut names and prices, coffee options, and more. The one that hung directly over the racks of donuts on display, in full view of all the customers, illuminated from behind, casting a giant silhouette of the tiniest mouse—no bigger than the end of my thumb—that appeared whenever I cranked the radio, and that seemed to dance along with me, racing from end to end, jumping up and down, just daring anyone who came in to notice and to make him stop.

But nobody seemed to notice.

I would stand between the front counter and the back row of donuts, box held in my left arm, cradled like a baby, tissue in my right hand, at the ready to snatch up a customer's selections, pop it into the box, and send them on their way. All the while, just over my head, that little silhouetted mouse seemingly did everything in his power to draw attention to himself.

It amazed me just how much people missed—couldn't or wouldn't see—even if it was staring them in the face.

Maybe my mouse was trapped. Maybe he had gotten in there through some hole and couldn't find his way out. Maybe he figured he had to get noticed and rescued by somebody or die from lack of water or food or from being so alone.

However he came to be, and whatever his intent, I welcomed him, pretending he was mine.

The angel bells tinkled. The sun had set. Already, it was dark outside.

A man came in. He sported black, mop-like hair. He reminded me of Moe from *The Three Stooges*. He already had a box of the donut shop's donuts in his hands. He stepped up to the other side of where I was standing, only the cash register between us. He had a disgusted sort of smirk on his face. I was about to open my mouth, but he didn't give me time even to say, "May I help you?" He just tossed the dozen-donut box onto the counter and slid it toward me.

"I'd like to return these," he said. Calmly. Quietly.

We had never had a return of donuts before. At least not that I knew of.

"Return?"

The man raised his eyebrows and pointed to the box. Without his saying a word, I understood that he wanted me to look inside.

I did.

The dozen donuts weren't a full set any longer. Three or so were missing. Eaten, I assumed. It took me a few seconds to notice the buttermilk ball, a giant bite taken out of it. A giant bite that had just missed chomping the head off an equally giant cockroach that had accidentally been baked inside. (At least I knew it was accidental on the part of the cockroach. Unless maybe that was his dying wish, to be entombed in his version of heaven.)

I silently prayed my mouse wasn't dancing overhead. And if he was, I prayed this man wouldn't notice.

"So . . . ?" Moe was starting to show his anger.

I forced myself to stop thinking about the cockroach's final moments, even suppressing a bit of a chuckle about my mouse and the given situation, and went into girl-in-charge mode: apologizing; swearing this had never happened before—"it's not the way we run our shop"; forcing the cash register to open and pulling out dollars and change; giving him more of a refund than what he had paid;

offering him another dozen donuts of his choice to take home; asking him if he'd like the owner to contact him directly . . .

I represented the best in customer service.

He wasn't impressed.

He took the cash, dismissed everything I had said, and, with a wave of his hands, turned and walked out our front door. I was certain I would never see Moe again.

I looked back into the box. I figured I couldn't toss it yet. Mr. Kumar would require proof to explain away why the cash register was short by a few dollars.

I wondered if I had been the one to give Moe his cockroach delight. If I had, it wouldn't have been my fault. It's not like you could see the insect from the outside of that donut. No, it had been baked deep inside. And that made me suspicious, and made me wonder if it had been done on purpose.

I turned my head and looked up at the milk-glass prison of my mouse. Was he locked up there on purpose, too? I didn't see him at the moment. I turned the music up a little bit louder, hoping to coax him out.

The dough used for a buttermilk ball isn't like the dough used for a raised donut. The former is very thick, very dense; the latter is almost like pancake batter. I didn't know much about cockroaches. But what I did know included the following: they grossed me out, they were a sign of unsanitary conditions, they were fast, they came out at night, and they scattered the second the lights were turned on. What I didn't know was whether they could burrow through what probably would be like hardening cement for a human, and whether they'd even want to. It seemed to me that the answer was no.

I came to my own conclusions. One of the Mr. Kumar–cloned bakers must have grabbed that cockroach, forced him into a ball of dough, and, before he could wriggle his way free, plunged him into one of the vats of bubbling, frying oil.

Disgusting.

Who would do such a thing? I wondered.

I wondered if any of the other bakers had seen him do it. Had they laughed about it? Had they done it and then watched that specific donut to see who would end up getting it?

Suddenly a thought popped into my head: Had they done it in hopes that it would be *me* who ate it? Buttermilk balls were my all-time favorite. Everybody who knew me knew that. And when the bakers brought out a fresh batch, I always snuck in and double-glazed them, or at least double-glazed the ones I wanted to take home.

Did they hate it when I did that? Were they trying to teach me a lesson?

I tried not to think of the possibility. I had thought I was pretty well liked at the donut shop. Even by Mr. Kumar.

I didn't want to think about it any longer.

I took the box with the cockroach donut, walked into the back room, scribbled a note to Mr. Kumar right on the box, and left it on the table, where I was sure he would see it.

I was headed back out to the front when the angel bells announced somebody's arrival. I quickly moved through the baking room and turned into the front room. I crossed the threshold from back room to front, and then I stopped.

Gunner.

He was standing there. Not sitting on his usual pink stool at the counter. Not waiting on the other side of the lowboy glass case. Not standing just inside the doors, finishing up a call on his police radio.

He was standing behind the front counter. In between the donut displays and the cash register. On my side of the counter. Just inches from me.

He had never crossed that line before.

"Do me a favor, would ya?"

That's how it started. That's what he wanted.

He wasn't really even looking at me.

He was pulling lengths of Scotch tape from the dispenser, the one we used to seal donut boxes by the dozen. He was acting as if he belonged there. In my space. Where I worked. Uninvited.

He even grabbed himself one of the strawberry-iced donuts he loved so much, with his bare hand, right from the display rack, stuffing it in one bite into his mouth and seeming to swallow it whole.

"Hey." I didn't know what else to say.

If I had known what else to say, I would have said something like, "Hey, this area is for employees only—don't make me call the cops," or "Preferred customers belong at the front of the store," or "If you're on this side of the shop, I'm putting you to work," or "Don't think I'm splitting my tips with you—back over there you go!" or something, anything, to make him realize he was where he did not belong.

He had taken those strips of tape, each about a foot long, and started lining them up, affixing just the top edge of each along the glass counter, letting them dangle like streamers hanging off the handlebars of the bicycle I rode when I was little.

I just watched, almost mesmerized, paralyzed.

He walked backward, still facing me, to where the coffee pot and mugs were. He had been served enough times to know how to serve himself, if he wanted to, and he did.

He returned with the hot coffee, pausing just a moment in his step to grab the sugar dispenser from the counter and quick-pour two shots of it into his cup. He came back to where I stood, still in the same spot. He took a gulp of his drink, set the cup down on the top of the glass, and returned to his project at hand.

He didn't ask.

He just reached out and pulled my hands toward him. He lifted my arms, bending them at the elbows, and positioned my hands in front of his chest, as if he would be placing handcuffs around my wrists. With one hand of his holding one outstretched hand of mine, he took those long strips of tape—sticky side up—and began wrapping them over and over my hands, from the tips of my fingers to the base of my palms.

He didn't give me a chance to ask what he was doing, but the look on my face must have been clear enough to ask the question on its own.

"I need your help in getting rid of 'the evidence,'" he said, smiling, while arching his back a little and showing off his body.

That's what he called it. The evidence.

I knew Gunner had cats. I had known ever since he'd told me during our first meeting. And even if he hadn't told me, the number of times he had come into the shop with cat hair visible on his uniform (which was tight against his body) were too many to be counted. Anybody paying even the slightest bit of attention could see the cat hair that covered him.

I relaxed a little. This was just me again, being me. Gunner just needed a friend to help him brush off all that hair. He probably didn't even notice how bad it was until he got in here, under these lights.

I looked up at the milky-white glass. Still no mouse.

He pulled me by my waist just a little bit closer to him. My hands were now fully wrapped up, like those of a mummy. I couldn't help but feel as if my tongue had been cut out, just like what I'd learned in school they did to people before wrapping them up like mummies. I didn't understand why I couldn't think of a thing to say. I thought about that line "cat got your tongue," and, as funny as it might have been, given the situation, I found no humor in it.

Gunner placed my taped-up hands, palm-side down, onto his chest. His hands guiding mine, he began to use me to stroke him. It was the first time I had ever had my hands on a guy's chest, let alone anywhere else. Not even my *papà* or my brother had I ever touched, not like this. It was the first time I'd really even touched Gunner anywhere, other than maybe his arm or his hand or something while he sat at the counter and we talked.

Gunner had always given me the "jumblies."

This was that. But it was also something more.

"This is what happens when you love your cats," he said, pulling my hands off him when the tape covering them had become overrun with fur and no longer able to do the job. "Thank you for helping me with my pussy problem."

To be honest, I have no clue if back then I knew what that word meant. Maybe I did. I just don't know. And whether or not I did, I can't be certain it would have mattered, not for any other reason than that I just don't think I was fully putting two and two together and equating the word with me.

But I don't know.

Gunner restrung the tape and rewrapped my hands, pressing them and dragging them over and over again down his chest, then his arms, then his thighs. When they became full of cat hair, he'd stop, repeat his process, replace the tape on my hands, then continue, even turning his back to me and asking me to get that, as well as the backs of his legs and his buttocks.

I did as he wanted.

My hands were at his mercy. So was my mind. He taught me how to stroke nearly every inch of his entire body, under the guise of ridding him of cat hair.

It didn't last long—not that time, nor all the times that followed. Just long enough to do the job. Not long enough to linger.

Still, if I was honest with myself, I admitted just how much it—all of it—excited me. I loved pressing my hands against him, the feel of his muscles moving beneath my touch. The thought of what I was actually touching.

Sometimes he'd laugh. "Hey, you missed a spot."

Sometimes it was just sounds he made, or silence between us.

I knew enough to know the feeling I was feeling. Down there. Without even having touched myself. And I knew enough to know that, regardless of what it looked like, of what conclusions some may have made, I was in way over my head and way out of control, and had no real clue as to what I was even doing.

Later that night, after Gunner had been swept clean of cat hair and had left to go wherever he called home—acting as if he had stopped in only for the usual chat, donut, and coffee visit—I had precious little time to myself before Papà came to pick me up. Already, I had gone to the restroom to pee and wipe not only my privates but also the inside of my panties. I worried about the stains; I knew

Mamma checked and might notice and would definitely interrogate me if she did.

Did this happen to everyone? I knew enough to know it happened with touch—but did normal people make it happen just by thinking bad thoughts? Did Gunner know this happened? To me? That he was the cause of it? Did it happen to him, too?

Or had I just imagined all of this?

The way Gunner had just left, like it was no big deal . . . maybe it was just that.

Another tinkling of the angel bells. My time to think in the bathroom was cut short. It could have been my *papà* arriving, or another somebody wanting something. I wished for it to be the latter. I wasn't yet ready to see my *papà* or for him to see me.

I quickly washed my hands, grabbed a paper towel, pushed open the door, and walked out and all the way around the perimeter of the serpentine counter, apologizing to the man who had come in with his preschooler and was waiting patiently at its edge. The donut shop only had one bathroom, and there was no backroom way to get to it, so everybody always knew your business. I always made sure, however, to exaggerate the wiping of my hands on that paper towel whenever coming out, since I was possibly being seen by customers. I wanted to make sure they knew I was clean.

I smiled as I passed the little boy, no more than four or five years old, who was playing on his own, right next to the pink stool Gunner sat on during his visits. I wondered if he would no longer take that seat. The little boy stomped about, sort of singing to himself, while I rounded the corner to go behind the counter, where Gunner and I had just been, and began helping his daddy pick out donuts.

I hadn't given a thought to cat hair flying around food.

And I had forgotten all about my mouse holed up in his silhouetted house.

Until the little boy suddenly started crying. His daddy looked at me and then over to him. I peered over the lowboy glass display to try and see what was happening. The boy pointed to his shoe. Something was stuck under it.

His daddy asked to be excused from me; I circled around the counter to the front as well, to see for myself. I had a horrible feeling, and I prayed that the little boy had not accidentally crossed paths with my tiny mouse.

My heart sank to see what was partially stuck to the bottom of his shoe. His daddy kept saying, "Oh my God," in between a half-laugh and a half-choking kind of sound. And the little boy kept repeating, "I sorry, I sorry."

I had no choice but to say it was okay, even though it really wasn't.

I helped with the cleanup. It seemed to be my role that night. I knew the little boy had not intended to hurt my little mouse. I could not say the same about the intentions of the adults that evening: the donut bakers or the cop.

The man with his son changed his mind about buying donuts that night.

And while I really could not be sure that night that it was my mouse, it would become clear to me that it was, given that I never again saw him behind the milk-glass sign. He, like me, had obviously made errors in judgment about when to be seen and when to remain hidden.

Surgery

I was starting to have an even harder time focusing. At home, at work, in school. My thoughts were having trouble keeping straight. I'd hopscotch from one thing to another, never finishing, or more like just forgetting, whatever train of thought I was on. Everything, especially thoughts about Gunner, seemed to be trying to muscle out everything else that was already fighting to be heard in my head. And now I was battling thoughts about yet another something I didn't quite understand. Nor was I sure I really wanted to.

Exploratory brain surgery.

It sounded so exotic, like a treasure hunt—pirates exploring uncharted territories.

But I knew differently.

I had to work on a research paper in school. Out of the thirty or so kids in our entire eighth-grade class, I had been chosen to represent St. Peter in a competition organized by the Catholic Church. The topic I was to write about was abortion. More specifically, I was expected to expose the evil truth that the word "abortion" really meant "killing babies." Didn't matter what *I* really thought about it. And, in truth, I didn't know what I thought about it. I really didn't ever think about it.

All I did think about was how much I hated research.

Research involved going to the library, looking up topics in the card catalogs, writing down numbers that made no sense to me at all, then finding those numbers that hopefully matched up with books that sat on some shelf in some corner of some too-darkly-lit floor in some too-quiet library. *If* the books were there and had not already been checked out by some other somebody who happened to be interested in your same interests at the very same time, then research involved either actually taking those books to some table in the library or checking them out for a limited amount of time, lugging them home, and actually reading through them in hopes of finding what might be some snippet of information relevant to the topic being researched that would merit inclusion in the paper being written.

I hated research.

Mr. Jaminez said, "Don't think of it as 'research,' Paolina; think of it as 'e-x-p-l-o-r-a-t-i-o-n.'" He stretched out that last word, excitedly gesturing with his hands in the air all around him to indicate, I assumed, the "out there" to be explored.

I tried. But I still hated it, no matter what it was called.

In Mamma's case, I hated the thought of her kind of e-x-p-l-o-r-a-t-i-o-n even more, because the "out there" to be explored was actually "in there."

As in, *in her head.*

Somehow, just the size of the terrain to be explored made it pretty clear, at least to me, that there was little room to poke around and fumble, and lots of room to make irreversible errors.

Her head wasn't like my research paper on abortion, the first draft of which included a line I wrote that said something like, "The work the Catholic Church is already doing to save our children leaves much to be desired." That line had Mr. Jaminez doubled over in laughter, telling me that what I wrote meant the exact opposite of what I had intended to say. *That* error was easily corrected. But that wouldn't be the case if the doctors touched, cut, or took out the exact opposite of what they intended from somebody's brain.

Even after Mr. Jaminez's review and revisions, my research paper on abortion did not win grand prize in the competition. I only placed, and I can't remember if I got second or even honorable mention. Didn't matter, really. While it meant something to St. Peter's—they praised me publicly and promoted the school as a result—it meant nothing to me. Just one more assignment, one more expectation, to cross off my to-do list.

The one thing that that research project and abortion competition did do was make me wonder further about all the possible outcomes of Mamma's surgery.

Not that anybody sat us down to tell us of those possibilities. I'm sure they told Mamma and Papà. The doctors and hospital would have had to, I think. But the only thing my siblings and I were told was when and where it would take place. And we weren't really told what "it" was, exactly. Or when "it" would be over. Or what constituted a "win." Or whether there were first-, second-, and third-place outcomes. Or what would happen if *they* failed. Would *we* automatically lose?

The one thing we *were* promised was that this would be the ultimate fix. These saints would figure out the miracle cure, the end to all of Mamma's pain.

So said Papà.

I was curious what they would find inside her head when they opened her up. What were they even looking for? Would they know it when they saw it?

Curiosity kills the cat kept echoing in my brain as I stood in the doorway of our home, alongside the rest of my siblings, waving good-bye to Mamma and Papà that subzero day in December of '78. "Frigid." That's the word I kept hearing whenever anybody talked about the weather. That and "more snow." We'd already had to shovel the snow at least a couple of times. All I really wanted to do in that moment was shut the door, get back to where it was warm, and get on with my end-of-year school projects that were due, regardless of whether or not I might wake up in the next day or two to find out I no longer had a *mamma*.

True, sometimes I wished I didn't have one. Or at least not this one. But I took back all those wishes the minute I made them, every time, choosing to focus on the Mamma who made my favorite *pasta fina-fina* for dinner; or who traced swirls with her nails on my back, soothing me while we waited out a thunderstorm together; or who sewed little bells on the underskirt of a flower-girl dress she'd designed and was making for some important somebody's daughter. I chose that Mamma, rather than the Mamma who sometimes didn't say a word for days; or the one who refused to bathe; or the Mamma who stayed locked in her bedroom under the covers, talking nonsense in whispers, fearful that her every move was being recorded and that computers were controlling her or spirits or other evil things were stalking her.

No one knew what was going on. No one outside the family.

House rules. *Cosa nostra.*

Even inside, we weren't entirely sure ourselves of what was really going on. Which is why none of our teachers knew about Mamma having surgery; if they did, they might have had some understanding of why we kids might have seemed distracted as a result, and not in the right frame of mind to study, do our homework, and perform in the classroom.

I'm sure it would have helped my little sister, Viny, if her teachers had known. Painfully shy, borderline "normal" in terms of IQ, according to some test they made her take, and pretty much friendless, she suffered most of all. It would be years, however, before we would realize to what extent.

If teachers and others did know what was going on, though, there would have been more questions—questions that Papà wouldn't have been able to answer, even with my help—and we couldn't have that.

I thought about how Papà had orchestrated this surgery all on his own. Part of me was grateful for not having been burdened with the research it would have required. Part of me felt ashamed for letting him continue down this path without having researched it and without having advised him. Even though he did not ask for my help,

I felt as if I had abandoned him. I could have—should have—offered my help. I always had in the past. I wondered if I didn't this time because I, too, felt abandoned by him.

I didn't want to think about it.

But the voices in my own head were already at war.

If anything goes wrong, it's your fault. You know that, right?

I'm not to blame.

You should have volunteered to help.

I wasn't asked to get involved. He thinks he can do it without me.

Your mamma *could die.*

Not my fault. I had nothing to do with this.

I wondered if this was normal. Talking to myself. Arguing with myself.

I told myself to shut up. And I wondered if this—whatever it was that Mamma had wrong with her—was how it had started.

Before the explosion of episodes involving voices and paranoid delusions and a threatening rage, Mamma's troubles came in small, almost undetectable doses. We never wholly put two and two together. Or maybe we didn't want to. Neither did the doctors, it seemed. Or maybe they didn't know to. Because rather than seek or be directed to psychiatric answers, we pursued or were instructed to pursue physiological solutions.

Hence the exploratory surgery.

In short, Mamma was a guinea pig. And she went to the slaughter willingly. Anything to free her from what she described as "spiders in her skull and under the skin of her face."

I had seen someone else scratch at her own skin once before, screaming, "Get them off!"—similar to what Mamma said she felt on her own. But that was on TV. The same year I was seduced by *Rocky* at the movies, I was terrorized by a girl named *Sybil*. I remember being glued to the set, watching Sally Field portray a girl whose *mamma* abuses her to the point that she develops multiple personalities. I remember everybody talking about it at the time. I remember how shocking it was. How that girl grew up to be a bunch of different people all in one, and at any given time, you never knew who among the many characters who lived inside her head would show up to take care of whatever situation she'd found herself in.

I thought about it a lot when Mamma headed off to the University of Chicago for her exploratory surgery. But I said nothing. It wasn't the same as what we were experiencing. And even if it was, I'm not sure we or anybody at that time would have admitted it. Or known what to do about it.

It was one thing to have something physical out of whack. A fractured bone. A kidney stone. A heart attack. In the late 1970s, people understood and knew how to deal with these physical ailments. Doctors knew how to treat and repair them. As with a mechanic's body shop, there were manuals to follow that allowed you to drive in broken and drive out fixed.

But the brain as a body part didn't make it easy for anybody to get familiar with all of its moving parts. And the mind, not the physical organ but the parts that go even deeper, the ones connected to thoughts and feelings and the soul and things that maybe even today nobody knows, *that* was still a complete mystery.

That year, 1978, it seemed as if the closer we got to Mamma's surgery, the more the TV kept bombarding me with people and stories and situations that brought into question and into mainstream conversation minds that had gone mad.

Serial killers were front and center because of Ted Bundy, the Hillside Strangler, and the Son of Sam. John Wayne Gacy probably haunted me the most. Maybe because he was from Chicago. Maybe because those images of him dressed as a clown, playing with all those little boys as if he was their friend, their guardian, hit home on an added front. It also was the year of Jim Jones's mass murder-suicide. His powerful mind convinced the majority of something like nine hundred people to drink a deadly Kool-Aid mixture and end their own lives. I could not shake the photos of those children with their own *mammas*, all facedown, arm in arm.

Head cases. Each one believing whatever stories their minds spun. Whatever voices they heard. Whatever versions of the truth they chose.

How did they get that way? Were they born with some glitch in their brains? Was it hereditary? Did somebody do something to them to make them what they had become? Or was it all just random, and any one of us could crack at any time?

I found myself wondering where I fit on the spectrum. What rested along that continuum of crazy? Where did Mamma fit? Was Gunner on it? The doctors who thought it a good idea to split open a skull and explore? The Catholic Church and teachers who thought it a great idea to host a middle-school writing competition about abortion? At what point were the things your mind told you significant enough to make you "not normal," to push you over the edge, to label you a bona fide head case? And at what point did people even notice?

I did not know. Nor did I have any desire yet to research it and figure it out.

I just prayed to God that Mamma would come home, her exploratory surgery pronounced a success, her head bandaged up, and that whatever part of her was broken would finally be fixed.

"Can I tell you something?"

I had just exited the bathroom stall at St. Peter's. The bathrooms on the third floor were pretty much exclusive to the seventh and eighth graders, given that we were the only two classes on that floor. At ten, I was one of the first to have gotten my period—and for the better part of two years, all of my classes were on the second floor, where the fourth, fifth, and sixth grades were. The second-floor bathrooms didn't offer sanitary-napkin dispensers. I didn't carry a purse, and starting would have been a dead giveaway. The girls' uniforms didn't have pockets, and my hands were too little to conceal something that was pretty much the size of a hoagie roll, so I panicked monthly, not only for fear of accidentally leaking and everybody seeing, but also because I had to figure out how to race upstairs to use those bathrooms, praying I'd make it back downstairs in time for my next class, and, hopefully, do it all without anybody's really noticing what I was doing or why.

I failed more often than not.

Angela Garnet was asking if she could tell me something. Alone. Just the two of us. In the bathroom. Angela was one of my sweetest and prettiest classmates, in a girl-next-door kind of way. Her big blue eyes and thick blond hair were born of German descent; her parents had literally run away from Hitler to start a new life in America. Angela had something like eight siblings, and each one looked distinctly like "one of the Garnets." Angela was in every way a carbon copy of her mother. Every birthday, Angela's mom would send her to school with giant homemade cupcakes with buttercream frosting that swirled all around the top and always ended with a tiny curled peak that seemed to defy gravity and stay suspended in the air, regardless of how the sun or the school's indoor winter heaters threatened to melt them.

I loved those cupcakes. I always wondered how her mom got that frosting so perfect. And I really liked Angela. But it wasn't as if we talked, or hung out in the same circle of friends.

I nodded in response to her request, making my way to the sink to wash my hands.

She hesitated a bit and then said, "This isn't easy to say, but I think you should know. Before any more kids start talking."

I could hear my heart pounding louder and louder.

"You smell." She just blurted it out and then continued to ramble about how she wasn't trying to hurt my feelings, she was trying to help, how my hair had become so greasy, especially lately, and everybody was noticing . . .

I stopped hearing what she was saying. I didn't respond. I don't think I even noticed her leave. I just stood there, the water dribbling from the faucet and hitting the sink, the sound echoing in my head. I couldn't even look at myself in the mirror.

I smelled.

When? When had I started to smell? To look "greasy"? How long had everybody been talking about me? Did I smell at the donut shop, too? Did Gunner notice? Oh God. How embarrassing. What was wrong with me? What was wrong in my head that I didn't even notice and do something about it? Was this another sign of my being further down my *mamma's* path than even I had realized? Was I, too, a head case?

Mamma had for a while now refused to bathe. She smelled. She tried to cover it up sometimes with her favorite perfume, Tabu, but then her body odor just smelled French. Like it should be called "body *odour*" or something. It was so bad that I hated to kiss her good night or good morning. But I still did it. We all did. And I never told her she smelled. None of us did.

I raced home and locked myself in the bathroom. I usually took baths, not showers, and, truthfully, didn't wash my hair more than once or twice a week. It wasn't just because Mamma said we didn't need to. And it wasn't because I thought hidden cameras were snapping pictures of me naked in the bath, which is the reason Mamma gave us for why she wasn't bathing regularly. I didn't like showers, and I didn't wash my hair as often as I should because I was afraid to. Afraid of the water.

It happened when I was eight, not yet in the third grade. We lived at the house on Chase Street, still in Skokie. It was a short, squat, light-colored brick bungalow that sat unassumingly in the middle of the block and sported a flower bed in front that was full of multicolored petunias all spring and summer long. It also had a yard in back, big enough for a swing set. We all loved that house. Uncle Joe, Mamma's brother, lived in it with us.

Summers were always hot and humid in Illinois, and that August of 1973 had the added challenge of those seventeen-year cicadas and the deafening noise that came with them. You couldn't really see them, but you could hear them—sort of like a mixture of screeching and whistling and the world's largest aerosol can being sprayed in an echo chamber underwater. And you couldn't stop it. It felt as if these bugs were just revving their engines louder and louder until one day they'd attack, like those Hitchcock birds. But they never did. These things were smarter—they knew they could drive you insane with just sound.

We longed for some distraction. Anything that would drown out that constant buzzing.

Mrs. Rowan, who lived on our block, knew just what to do. She invited all the kids over for a pool party. Not only would having a bunch of kids splashing around cool us all off and give us something to do, but she didn't have kids, so it would bring the sounds of children playing to her for at least an afternoon.

We begged Mamma to let us go. She wasn't a fan of the water, but she had little strength to argue with all three of us at once. So Cathy and Ross and I were allowed to attend, even though not a single one of us knew how to swim. Viny stayed home.

I wasn't afraid of the water back then. I loved playing in the sprinklers or sitting in the little pool in our backyard, as long as my feet were firmly planted on solid ground.

We all jumped into Mrs. Rowan's pool. It was aboveground and was at least four feet deep. My brother and sister were both taller than I was, so when they were in the pool, their feet touched the bottom, at least enough for them to be in there on their own. I did not know this important fact. What I did know was that I was forced to wear some kind of smelly plastic donut thing around my middle, and that, in my opinion, was not fair. What I neglected to take into account was that that unfair inner tube was designed to keep me afloat and alive.

While everyone splashed around, laughing and having fun, I let go of my lifesaver, slipped right through it, and sank to the bottom. I suppose I would have come up shortly thereafter had I only kept my mouth closed. Unfortunately, as I sank and saw everyone's legs moving around underwater, I opened my mouth and shouted out, "Help me."

Nobody heard. And I went unnoticed.

When I woke up, I was lying on the ground just outside the pool. It seemed everybody in the neighborhood was standing around me. Mrs. Rowan was crying. Mr. Rowan was kneeling beside me, looking scared and as if he were waiting for me to speak and say something profound. It dawned on me that I must have died, for just a little bit, that day. And later, when Mamma said we would never be allowed back into any pool ever again, and when the Rowans announced that children would no longer be allowed in their pool ever again, I think I died a little bit more. I was sure that all the kids blamed me, hated me for ruining their summer fun.

Days later, when Mamma tried to wash my hair, the sensation of water rushing over my head and into my eyes and ears sent me into a panic, so much so that I refused even to wash my hair. My *papà*, being a barber who was used to washing people's hair, decided he would give it a try, reassuring me that he would not get any water in my ears or eyes.

He lied.

I'm sure he tried as best he could, but my trembling with fear and not keeping still made his promise impossible to keep. He even tried to put masking tape over my eyes so I wouldn't see what was coming. It didn't do the trick. Instead, not seeing freaked me out even more. I thrashed and pulled away and screamed and cried. As I tried to run away from him, his empathy turned to anger and escalated. His solution to the problem? His belt. Repeatedly, he struck me—not just on my fanny, but everywhere. He couldn't help it, given how much I was squirming to get away. My legs, my back, my chest, my head. Everywhere.

My siblings watched from the laundry chute, which gave them a clear view from the upstairs down to where I was. They knew not to get involved. Mamma did, too. But at one point, probably when she realized that I would soon be beaten to death and she would be burying a child and visiting a husband in prison, she stepped into harm's way, putting herself between me and Papà. I fell to her feet, clinging to her as my only possibility for survival. She raised an arm to Papà and commanded, "*Basta!*" Enough. One word, and he snapped to. Mamma never raised her voice to Papà. The hitting stopped immediately. Had it not, without doubt, I would have been dead.

I silently thanked God that Mamma had found her voice.

The next day at school, I could not breathe. I went to the nurse's office. She called Mamma, who then called Papà to come get me. I wonder what the school officials must have thought, seeing all those bruises. I wonder why no one said a word. It was as if it were perfectly normal to see a kid with visible welts. Maybe it was.

As I sat in the nurse's office, I managed to convince the nurse that it would be easier if I waited outside for Papà, English not being his first language and all. She allowed it. Little did she know, I had other plans. The moment I exited the building, I was going to keep on going. No clue to where. My plan wasn't that well thought out, but I was running away. It would be the first of many times I had enough.

I pushed open the double glass doors. I struggled to inhale the fresh air. My chest was so bruised, it hurt just to breathe. Almost as if in slow motion, I turned to assess which way I would run, only to see, turning the corner, our white Pontiac. The realization deflated me. The second I was free, Papà had already arrived.

The car raced toward me and jerked to a stop. Papà exited and nearly stumbled to reach me. He put one arm around my back, and with his other, he gently took my hand in his. I remember looking up at him, into his face. He had tears in his eyes. I don't think I had yet seen him cry. Immediately, I wanted to tell him, *It's okay, it's my fault, I'm so sorry I'm so bad.* But I didn't. I was as exhausted as a child of that age could be. And I sank into his strong arms. Papà picked me up and carried me to the car. He eased me into the passenger seat.

Seat belts weren't a concern back then, so I curled up like a pill bug and shut my eyes.

We entered the offices of our family physician, Dr. Tazinelli. I loved Dr. Tazinelli. He was a doctor, but not the kind a kid fears. Sure, he gave shots, but the way he did it, you barely noticed. He was a giant. He had to duck to clear the top of the doorway to enter a room. His hair was shiny black and slicked back, like Frank Sinatra or Dean Martin or the singers we watched on *The Lawrence Welk Show* every Sunday night. His hands were bigger than my head. I know because when he made a house call once when I was very sick, he put his whole hand over my face to feel for a fever. His hand was so warm and welcoming. I wanted to crawl up into it and ask him to take me with him. Dr. Tazinelli never hurt little girls. And before he said good-bye to you, he always gave you yummy suckers with the loopy strings as handles.

I remember the look on his face as he looked at me and then at my *papà*. It was a look of disapproval and disgust. Papà broke down and could barely choke out the truth of what he had done. He swore it would never happen again. And, to that extent, it never did.

Angela's words stung. But, as I had learned time and time again, I needed to just pretend it hadn't happened. True, I needed to pay attention and *not* do ever again whatever I had done to cause it to happen—to ensure that it would never happen again—but aside from that, I just needed to stuff it down with everything else. That way, it couldn't hurt me anymore. I avoided looking at myself in the mirror. I swore right then and there that I would bathe every night and every morning. And I would wash my hair every other day at a minimum. And I would force myself to put my whole head directly under the shower's spray, no matter how scared I was.

That night, I started the water running. I stripped down and stepped into the tub. I quickly pulled the little knob that diverted the water from the faucet at the bottom to the shower at the top and jumped back, out of the way of the spray. My body trembled, and I was panting. I could feel again the water over my head, in my ears, nobody hearing me cry for help. I needed to talk myself into moving and standing underneath that showerhead. I turned around, so as not to face it, and slowly—it must have taken me at least fifteen minutes—backed up into the water. The moment it hit the back of my head, I could barely stand it. The water rushing over and into my ears nearly made me scream, forcing me to put one hand over my mouth. I kept it there, and I continued to back up. As the water began falling over the front of my face, I squeezed my eyes as tightly as I could and put my other hand over my nose. I tried to breathe through my mouth and kept repeating Angela's words: "You smell. You smell. You smell." I knew that would force me to do what I had to do. And it did.

I also started praying harder. "Please, God, help me be more normal than not. Please don't make me a carbon copy of Mamma."

Surprises

There was something wonderfully warm about the donut shop in the winter. Every one of my senses felt heightened by it. From the minute I arrived, standing in front of the door, I purposely exhaled just before opening it, and then inhaled as deeply as I could as soon as I crossed the threshold. I loved breathing in the icing and dough-frying scents of sweet treats that during that time of year seemed to smell even sweeter. Even the fresh coffee brewing smelled stronger, as if it had a little more kick in it to help jump-start a body on such cold, cold mornings.

During the holiday season, Mr. Kumar would try to incorporate red and green into whatever frostings he could, not because he was filled with the Christmas spirit but because he was trying to boost profits by masking day-old donuts and fooling customers into believing they were buying something festive and "limited time only." He even displayed them in the specialty case or just behind the label TODAY'S SPECIAL. Everybody wanted one. They were pretty much the very same donut (only less fresh) a customer might have among what he had already chosen in his box of a dozen. But with the sexier outer shell and a "surprise" for a name, they couldn't tell, and they just *had* to have one.

As much as that should have bothered me, it didn't. While I had to stop myself from thinking about the real reason those donuts existed, I couldn't help but love the sight of all that Christmas red and green. And while working a holiday might have bothered some people, I didn't mind. Christmas Eve fell on a Sunday in 1978, and I got to work it during the day, given that was my usual shift. In a lot of ways, it felt more like Christmas at the donut shop than it did at home. All day long, so many more people than usual came into the shop, nobody really caring about diets, most people smiling and wishing one another—whether they knew each other or not— "Merry Christmas!" or "Happy holidays!" And the tips were more than usual, especially from the regulars.

Ron was one of my favorite regulars. A leather-faced, black, grandpa-like trucker, he always came in, day or night, shouting out his order as he walked his way to his usual spot, the farthest stool along the counter.

"Hey, sweetheart," he'd call out to me in a voice that sounded like gravel. "Whatever soup smells best to you, and you know what else."

He always said the same thing. And he always called me sweetheart. And almost always, before he was settled onto his stool, I already had his cup of coffee (black) and donut (an old-fashioned formed with a handle ready to dunk) placed in front of him. Sometimes I was fast enough and he was slow enough for me to even beat him to his seat with a bowl of piping-hot chili or stick-to-your-ribs beef barley. As much as Ron always said I could choose whatever soup I wanted to give him, and always ate whatever I served him, I could tell that these two varieties were his favorite, and I always made sure we had one or the other among our three offerings. I also made sure we always had chicken noodle, but that was for me, because it was *my* favorite.

I watched outside our floor-to-ceiling windows, ice framing the corners and the inside heat fogging up my full view. I loved seeing those little swirls of steam trailing behind coffee-drinking customers as they jogged through the snow and cold from our front door and back to their parked-but-still-running cars. That's how cold it was that winter. We even had to keep jumper cables behind the front counter because, more often than not, people who turned their engines off had trouble getting them started again. Tonight, on top of the cold, my favorite weatherman, WGN's Tom Skilling, was forecasting snow. Maybe lots of it. That worried me a little bit because we were going to Aunt Rose and Uncle Sam's house to celebrate Christmas Eve. They lived on the South Side, near Midway Airport. Not only was it quite a long distance from where we lived in Skokie, but once you arrived, the neighborhood wasn't exactly welcoming. More like frightening. As in, you might get your Christmas presents stolen or you yourself might get shot.

I wondered why we were doing it. Mamma had gotten home from her exploratory brain surgery only a couple of weeks earlier, and she wasn't in great shape. As much as we all wanted to believe that her deteriorated condition was rightfully due to her having had such an invasive operation, I don't think a single one of us really believed that was the case. And I didn't think it was such a good idea for her to be exposed to such bitter cold. It was weird, too, because we usually didn't venture out to other people's homes for the holidays; they usually came to us. Papà did say that Uncle Sam, Mamma's baby brother, was such a scaredy-cat driver in good weather, and never arrived anywhere on time, that if he were to drive to us this winter, either he'd never make it or we'd be waiting until New Year's for he and Aunt Rose to arrive. It was safer, at least for them, to let my *papà* take all the risk.

There was something more, too—something else a bit odd, at least to me. Mamma really wanted to go. *Really.* And she never wanted to, not to spend time with her sister-in-law Aunt Rose. She avoided her like she avoided personal hygiene. Granted, Aunt Rose's entire side of the family would be there, and Mamma had been told how much everybody wanted to see her and find out how she was doing, but it felt more as if Mamma felt she was going to her coming-out party or something. She would be the center of attention, and it seemed as if she couldn't wait.

I shrugged off my fears and tried to excite myself with the

possibility of getting more presents, given it was Christmas Eve and Aunt Rose's entire family would be exchanging gifts. For our family not to receive anything to open that night would reflect poorly on that Sicilian family. I prayed they played by those same rules.

I also prayed that I would get to see Gunner to wish him a merry Christmas. I had thought about buying him a Christmas present but didn't really know what he might like. Some of the customers, the regulars, gave Karen and Aurora and me Christmas presents, though nothing big or expensive—at least mine weren't. My favorite gift to get was a scented candle. Aurora's seemed to be liquor. And Karen always seemed happiest to get envelopes. I never saw what was in those envelopes, but I figured her gifts were of the cash kind.

I wondered if Gunner would give me a gift. And if he were to give me one, I wondered what kind of gift he would think I would want to get. I secretly hoped that if he did give me something, he wouldn't give Aurora or Karen a present. Or at least not the same one. That would be worse. Maybe it was better if he didn't give anybody any gifts.

When Gunner and Officer Brown did show up that day, they did what they had been doing since it had turned so cold that winter: they drove up and not only kept their engine running but didn't even bother to lock their doors or park in actual spaces, between the lines, like everybody else had to do in the lot; instead, they just stopped their squad car parallel to our front windows, hopped out, came in, and immediately moved to the front of the line. Gunner always came in with Officer Brown during the day, but at night he almost always visited me solo.

"Merry Christmas, everyone!" they both said out loud, almost in unison.

I always tried to be the one to serve them when they came in. But more often than not, I'd get stuck taking somebody's order, usually somebody who had trouble making decisions. That's where I was that day while Aurora walked out from behind the counter, donuts and coffees already in hand, to do the honors.

"Ach! My two most handsome men in uniform. Come give Aurora her Christmas gift."

As she set the food and drink packages on top of the counter, she started with Officer Brown, throwing her arms around him and pressing herself up against him. She hugged and kissed him, but only on the cheek.

"If only you weren't married!" she said loudly, making everyone in the shop laugh.

Officer Brown batted his long lashes and feigned an "aw shucks" kind of motion. He picked up his coffee and started to sip, while, along with the rest of the shop, all attention now turned to Gunner.

"*You* are not married," Aurora said, wagging her finger as she shimmied her way to him.

Gunner playfully took a step back and put up his hands. "No, but I do have a girlfriend."

That didn't stop Aurora from practically tackling him. At least that's what it looked like to me. As she rubbed herself against him and kissed him full on the lips, her too-short skirt rose even higher in the back, exposing even more of her bare, shapely thighs.

While the crowd seemed pleased with the performance, which didn't seem to be coming to an end anytime soon, I couldn't stop thinking one thought: *I do have a girlfriend.* That's what he'd said. He'd never told me he had a girlfriend. He just said he had two cats. No girlfriend. Cats. And if he had a girlfriend, why wasn't he taping up *her* hands and having her help him with his "pussy problem"?

I wasn't paying attention to the slower-than-slow customer who was still in front of me and who a minute ago hadn't been able to make a choice and seemed to have all the time in the world and because of whom I ended up not being the one to serve Gunner on Christmas Eve, and now Aurora was all over him. But now she was wondering why I was taking so much time and saying she needed to go, could you hurry up, please, miss?

I so wanted to mouth off to her, but I said nothing. I taped shut her box, rang her up, took her money, handed her her donuts, and silently cursed her as she went on her way.

Aurora was finally starting to loosen her embrace, saying something about how she loved her "best Christmas present"; my eyes locked onto Gunner's at the exact time his locked onto mine, giving me an expression that sort of said, *What was I supposed to do?* And then he winked and smiled at me.

He separated from Aurora, moving away from her and closer to the counter and me.

"Santa got you down as naughty or nice this Christmas, *POWwwwleeena?*"

He picked up his donut bag and coffee, took a giant gulp, and hesitated for a second. I think he was actually hoping for an answer, but I was sort of shocked silent. I had still been thinking through the girlfriend comment, then had been sidetracked by his wink and that smile, and now I was getting hit with a question I didn't expect. And I didn't know what he would think of either answer. Naughty? Nice? I didn't have time to figure out what *I* wanted him to think. I opened my mouth, but I had no idea how to respond.

And that's when he winked again, this time giving me more of a wicked kind of smile, as if he were pleased with himself for flustering me in front of everyone. I knew everyone could see my red face, and I knew that's why they were laughing.

Officer Brown and Gunner left, shouting out a final season's greeting.

I turned my back to the crowd and checked on the donuts, pulling out a tray of something that really didn't yet need refilling and taking it into the back room to pretend to fill it. I tried not to think. Girlfriend? Did he really have one? Or did he look at me that way because I might be . . . ? What had he hoped I would answer? Naughty? Nice?

Mr. Kumar approached me and snorted. "Come on." He motioned for me to get back out front to help the still-swelling crowd. I tossed a couple more donuts onto the tray that didn't need it and did as he said. But for the remainder of my shift and well into the night, I couldn't stop thinking about Gunner.

"Paolamia, che pensi?"

I think my silence somehow made Papà uneasy. Whenever I was quiet, especially for extended periods, he always asked what I was thinking. We had been in the car now for nearly two hours. We were close to Aunt Rose and Uncle Sam's house, but the snow and the traffic meant that what would normally have taken five more minutes would probably end up being more like another fifteen to maybe even thirty. I had not said more than two words the entire time.

"Niente."

Make that three.

"Nothing." My usual response. I could see my *papà*'s eyes looking back at me, smiling at me, in the rearview mirror. I smiled back, hoping to reassure him.

I was sandwiched in the backseat between Ross and Cathy, while Viny sat in the front between Mamma and Papà. I was lost in my own thoughts, not contributing at all to whatever the conversation was that was taking place. Gunner consumed me. I wasn't even concerned any longer about Mamma and the Christmas Eve party.

But I should have been.

We had hoped Mamma's exploratory surgery would fix her and give her and us some peace—or, at the very least, some answers. But in the days following her return, it was clear that nothing had changed. In fact, it seemed only to get worse, as if a dial had immediately been turned to full blast. She seemed to see more things that weren't there, hear more voices that were speaking all sorts of evil. And to imagine more people, more plots, more paranoia-induced happenings with one single intent: to kill her.

And in her mind, we were in on it.

I wondered if anybody else in the family noticed. We all sort of whispered around Mamma, so I imagined we all knew, but we never said anything. We never compared notes. Not in the beginning. As in, the first several years.

We finally arrived at Aunt Rose and Uncle Sam's beige brick cookie-cutter home. It looked tiny from the outside, and it was exactly that on the inside. The only way they were able to fit nearly fifty people in that house was to stuff us all downstairs in what was a giant, unfinished concrete basement that ran the entire length of the structure. Uncle Sam had a very cool old-fashioned jukebox stationed right next to a bar he'd set up with pretty much every type of liquor imaginable. That's where I planned to spend my Christmas Eve, knowing I'd get served. It was one of the perks of being Sicilian: no real age thresholds to cross when it came to liquor.

I wondered how long it would take to get Mamma out of the car. It took at least fifteen minutes to get her in, and that was without a crowd of onlookers. She wore a very chic gray beret on her head, tilted to the side to cover her bandaged-up hole. She said it would protect her head, but it was made out of that soft, fuzzy sweater material angora, so I doubted it. She moved like a wind-up toy that was winding down. And we all surrounded her, supporting her, sort of like some queen's entourage or some presidential secret service escorting her in.

Once we finally made it to the front door, it seemed that everyone wanted to be the first to cross the threshold with Mamma on their arm. The grand entrance mattered. Pictures were being taken, and everyone seemed ready for their close-up. Bundled-up bodies fought with each other to squeeze through the narrow opening, almost knocking Mamma over in the process. Ross just shook his head. My uncle shouted out to all to clear the way. We now had to make it down a flight of concrete stairs. At this point, both Ross and I stayed behind, just listening to the commotion ahead, raising our eyebrows and rolling our eyes at one another, knowing that whatever we were imagining was probably not as hilarious as what was actually happening.

By the time we joined the others downstairs, Mamma was seated in an overstuffed armchair in the corner of the room farthest from the jukebox. All the noise proved to be a bit too much for her, and no sooner had she sat down and been greeted and fawned over by Aunt Rose's family members than she was ready to go.

I was ready to go, too. I looked around for Ross, noticing he was missing. As soon as I thought to head upstairs to search for him, however, I heard a booming voice from the top of the stairs, making its way down.

"Ho ho ho!"

Oh my God, no. As all the little kids in the basement squealed at the sound, I struggled to suppress my shrieks of equal parts horror and hilarity. Somehow, Aunt Rose had convinced my sixteen-year-old brother to dress up in full costume and play Santa. He was lugging a manila-colored sack filled with wrapped gifts that he was in charge of distributing, and wearing a full, fluffy white fake beard, matching bushy eyebrows, a double-pillow-stuffed red velvety suit, and even black oversize boots. My eyes connected with his. We both knew that he would never live this down. I would make sure of it.

While we each received something, Mamma got the most gifts. And with each one she was handed, she barely acknowledged it, needing help even to open it, and kept turning to Papà, telling him we needed to go.

"*Andiamo, Antonino. Andiamo!*"

And go we did.

I wondered why we had even bothered to trek all that way for nothing. I wondered why we did or did not do a lot of things. But I mostly kept my thoughts to myself. I had to admit, it was worth it to have witnessed Ross's humiliation, and it was comforting to be leaving so soon after we'd arrived, because that proved to me that Mamma was still the same Mamma, the one who held very little affection for crowds and sisters-in-law.

While Mamma remained constant, Papà seemed in an uncharacteristically foul mood all the way home during the car ride and even after. Before we went to sleep that night, I said to him the same line he always said to me: "*Che pensi, Papà?*"

He barely paused on his way up the stairs to say it, exhaling, completely deflated, telling me in less than a breath that he had asked Uncle Sam for a loan but Uncle Sam had said no. Then he quickly kissed me good night on my forehead, careful not to show me his face, and retreated to his bedroom, leaving me there with the news.

It dawned on me why Papà and maybe even Mamma had been so eager to go to Aunt Rose and Uncle Sam's house that night. And why we had left so quickly. We needed money. More money than Papà thought I or even Ross could help bring in. Uncle Sam had money. Lots of it. But he refused to help his sister and the mother of his goddaughter, me.

I hated him for it, for making Papà so sad he could not even look at me.

My mind traveled back to when I had been writing that research paper on abortion. I had told my *papà* about it. He had laughed and shaken his head, telling me that he thought it was bad, but maybe sometimes necessary, like when he and Uncle Sam had lived in Buenos Aires before coming to the United States. Almost without thinking what he was saying, Papà had told me that Uncle Sam had gotten some local girl pregnant, and because Uncle Sam hadn't had a job, Papà had ended up having to pay for the girl's illegal abortion. As soon as he'd said it, he'd told me to forget it. It was a secret he never should have shared.

I wished at that moment that I could have rewritten that paper and exposed the dirty secret. And hurt Uncle Sam as much as he had hurt Papà. Papà never should have said anything about needing money to an outsider. House rules. The fewer people who knew about things that could be used to hurt you, the better. I would have thought he would have kept to that. And I tried not to think about how bad our financial situation must be for him to purposely go against it.

I was determined to find more ways to make money to help Papà with whatever bills he had to pay.

On Christmas morning, I couldn't help but rejoice, realizing that I had made it well into the eighth grade. Just six more months until graduation. It wasn't the wearing of the cap and gown or the tassel transfer or the diploma delivery with handshake or even the "movin' on up" to high school that I celebrated. No, it was the fact that, despite everything going on, I would have escaped grade school without anyone knowing our secrets. As far as the community of St. Peter's knew, the Milanas were just some garlic-eating family who valued a good Catholic education and who attended Mass, at least on holidays.

No one knew about Mamma.

No one—no authority figure—knew I worked at the donut shop.

No one knew about Gunner.

No one knew much of anything about me.

And that kept me feeling safe and in control.

I don't remember opening gifts on that day. I'm sure we did. I don't remember what, if anything, we received. At most, we received one gift per kid. And during this time, we got even less, as Mamma's illness had sucked away any possible disposable income we might have had. We were used to it. Never said "boo" about it.

One Christmas—not this one—I remember we woke to find nothing under our tree; however, we did find Christmas cards—one addressed to each of us—hanging from its branches. Big, generic white envelopes. Cards, I'm sure, that depicted Baby Jesus in his mother's arms or the holy family in the manger or the three wise men following the star of Bethlehem—those were Mamma's favorites. The cards didn't have anything in them, nothing in the way of money. Or if they did, I'd venture to guess it was no more than a five-dollar bill—nothing memorable. That part, the part about what was in the cards, I can't remember, and it doesn't matter. What I do remember is how Papà took the time to handwrite personal notes to each of us. That was a true gift. Even at that young age, I knew how valuable it was.

On this particular Christmas morning, as we were rushing to get out of the house and off to morning Mass before all the seats were taken, something was different. From just after I woke, I could feel it. It was as if there were a presence looming, thick and heavy, wrapping itself around me like a cold chill. I instinctively needed us to get out of the house and on our way. It was a different sort of "jumbly"—something inside that screamed, *Danger, Will Robinson, danger.*

And there stood danger.

Mamma—dressed in Scarlett O'Hara red—appeared at the top of our stairs, the ones leading up from the split-level main floor where the living room and kitchen met the three bedrooms. One bedroom to the left was intended for Papà and Mamma to share, and they did, despite Mamma's having started to keep sharpened knives underneath the mattress and baseball bats underneath the bed as a real threat to Papà if he dared to step foot into the room, let alone sleep in the same bed with her. He refused to abide by her rules, and thus began the nights of Mamma sitting up all night in the living room, screaming profanities in Italian and swearing she would murder us all.

I had thought Mamma would be too tired from our Christmas Eve outing even to be awake. And she had pretty much stopped going to church altogether for a while now, despite how much Papà begged her to join him, so I just assumed we would be heading to Christmas Day Mass without her. When I saw her at the top of the stairs, all in red, the very color she never wore and would never have normally approved of, I knew that this was what I had been instinctively picking up on all morning. This was the danger to be feared.

Unfortunately, I could also see that what I saw as a red flag was, in my *papà*'s eyes, a Christmas miracle, because Mamma wanted to go to Mass with her family. She hadn't been to church since her head had started to hurt and the voices had started to speak and her delusions of seeing herself naked and fornicating with other men in national trade magazines had become just one of her many paranoid fears. To Papà, this was a sign that the surgery was working and that the daily novenas he prayed to Padre Pio—a *paisano* born in southern Italy and the first priest in the Catholic Church with the stigmata on his body—were finally being answered.

Papà, I had no doubt, was wrong.

The parking lot was blocked in; 10:00 a.m. Mass was the most popular on Christmas Day. Everyone we knew would be in attendance. All my friends from school. All my enemies. Our neighbors. Teachers. Everybody.

We sat in the back, taking up one of the few pews left open and able to accommodate a family of six. We greeted those sitting in the pews in front and behind. I waved nervously to a few friends who caught my eye. We followed along with the scripture. We sang the songs. We stood up to take communion.

I stood in front of Mamma. It made me nervous to have her behind me. I didn't know why, exactly, except that I didn't know what she was or wasn't capable of doing. I preferred to have her in my line of sight at all times. So I found myself turning my head to try and keep an eye on her. She smiled and nodded to the faithful in an eerie, "you just wait" sort of way. Papà stood behind her and winked and smiled reassuringly at me.

We finally reached Father Murgoff. "Body of Christ," he said to me as he moved his hand to place the host on my tongue.

"Amen," I replied, taking a sip of wine, turning quickly, and making my way down the long center aisle.

That's when it happened. My world became exposed. For not a moment later, I heard the screams—everyone heard them—echoing throughout the church. They came from Mamma. As parishioners got up off their knees, standing to see what was going on, I spun around and had a front-row view: there lay Mamma, in a heap, having thrown herself literally at the priest's feet, grabbing onto his legs as if they were buoys in a sea in which she was drowning. She began screeching more loudly, articulating for all to hear that we, her family, were trying to kill her.

Father Murgoff looked completely baffled, and then he looked at Papà, whose pleading eyes looked to me. I turned and walked down the aisle, avoiding anyone's gaze, and kept walking directly out the door.

The secret was finally out.

Stalkers

The phone rang. And rang and rang and rang. I refused to pick it up. And yet I couldn't stand the constant ringing. I knew who would be on the other end of the line. Well, maybe not "who," exactly, but I knew for sure what whoever was calling would be asking about: Mamma.

Already, the principal at school had phoned for Papà. Good thing I took that call. I had already mastered playing the role of *la piccola mamma*. I already wrote and signed notes and permission slips like a pro for myself and my siblings. Like a good consigliere for Papà, I had been able to postpone any kind of family counseling meeting until after the holidays, with every intention never to follow through.

I was relieved at how easy it was to keep them all at bay, as much as something inside me wished it wasn't.

The priests, the teachers, parents of the kids from school, friends—everyone wanting to know what the hell had happened, what was going on, was my mother really serious? A few wanted to know what they could do to help.

As if I really had answers.

I felt myself wanting to laugh. I kept trying to be serious, but the more I tried not to laugh, the worse the urge got, until it just bubbled up and out of me. I locked myself in the bathroom to laugh in private, covering my mouth and trying to drown out the sounds. Tears rolled down my cheeks. I just couldn't keep it in. I couldn't believe that what I had worked so hard to keep secret for so long was now out there. Everybody now knew. Everybody would be looking at me with that same look of pity, that look that said I had the cooties that nobody wants to catch.

It made me feel exactly like I was right back in the fourth grade, the year when I went into what I call "protective custody."

I was sitting in the back row of Ms. Pieri's homeroom class. I was pretty short for my age, and being squished into that little wooden desk made me look even tinier. I had to keep moving my head from left to right to see past the head of the classmate seated in front of me, just to read what was on the blackboard. When Mamma and Papà burst into the room, they looked panicked. The fact that they couldn't see me made it worse.

Mamma began shouting out, "*Dio mio, non c'e! Non c'e!*" I wasn't sure what Mamma meant by saying I wasn't there, but I knew something had happened and that it was serious.

"I'm here. I'm over here!" I stood up and waved my hand so they could see me. Mamma nearly collapsed into Papà's arms.

As I—and everyone at school—would learn, I had somehow attracted a stalker, before stalking was even popular. Some sick pervert had begun watching me, and as soon as I was out of the house and out of sight, he would phone Mamma and tell her exactly what I was wearing and how he had me tied up and how he was doing all these sexually perverse things to me.

That part wasn't true. That stalker had never touched me.

What *was* true was that there really *was* a stalker. The sad part of that story is real, and I so wish it wasn't. I wish I could say that it never really happened. I wish I could say that the stalker was all in Mamma's head, yet another delusion. I wish I could point to it as when things started down the path of crazy with Mamma, and then say that we just missed all the signs that built upon it. It would be so much easier if I could say that.

But I can't. And because it wasn't just in her head, but rather actual reality, it called into question, at least for me, what was real and what wasn't. Confirming the truth of my stalker gave credibility to Mamma, another damning piece of evidence proving that whatever was in me that Mamma believed was bad could, indeed, actually be. This stalker further convinced her that I was the root cause of all sexual deviation. Or at least it seemed to me that was what she thought, and how she made me feel.

Everyone knew about the stalker back then. The police were called in. And at St. Peter's, I was allowed on the playground during school recess only if teachers escorted and babysat me. I remember the kids in my class clasping hands and forming a protective shield around me.

Part of me felt embarrassed and under intense scrutiny for something I had done nothing to deserve, at least that I consciously knew of, while another part of me wished I could take them all home with me.

At the end, it turned out to be a seventeen-year-old who lived a few blocks away. Matt was his name. I knew who he was, but other than knowing that he was a bit of a bully and a degenerate and that he was the boy with the black hair that had a natural swatch of white tufted right in the front of his head—something he'd inherited from his mom, who had the same thing—I didn't know him at all.

That didn't stop Mamma from greeting me at home after school some days with a slap across my face. She never let me forget the incident, convinced that I had brought it on myself, given the way, she said, I conducted myself in public, especially when boys were around. I did not know what to think. About this stalker boy. About boys and me in general. About what Mamma would think. But, sadly, even though it didn't quite add up, as early as age ten, I was beginning to think that whatever Mamma thought, maybe she was right.

What I think scared me most about what Mamma did during Christmas services was that it made me doubt myself again. If the stalker incident was real, as crazy as it seemed, how did I know that what Mamma was experiencing now wasn't equally real? I know it's crazy even to think it. Logically, we weren't trying to kill Mamma. There were no hidden cameras. She had no spiders crawling under her skin and in her skull.

Right?

I wasn't entirely sure any longer.

What I was sure about was that I dreaded going back to school. As much as I dreaded staying at home. I thanked God we were on Christmas break. I stayed away from having contact with anyone from school or anyone who I thought might have been in church on Christmas Day as much as was possible. And I focused on the one place I still felt safe, the one place I felt bigger than myself: the donut shop.

I made a conscious decision to immerse myself in my work and make as much money as I could to help out Papà.

Mamma had made it clear—not open for discussion—that I was headed to the Catholic high school St. Scholastica, the same place Cathy already went. Not the free public high school, with boys included. No. I was destined for the expensive all-girls school. The one we couldn't afford. The one I had no desire to attend.

Cathy had been able to get financial aid. I wasn't sure I would. The school seemed to have an unwritten policy of granting financial aid to as many families as possible, so your chances lessened if you already had one girl in the family receiving assistance. I guessed the theory was that if a family already had one daughter enrolled, they'd experience way too much Catholic guilt to deny the daughters who followed the same education. Somehow, they'd find a way to pay.

Their theory seemed to be working, at least with us. Mamma didn't care what Papà had to say about our not being able to afford it. And she certainly wouldn't have wanted to hear me argue against a same-sex school. I could only imagine what kind of accusations and punishment saying something like that would bring me.

§

I asked for more shifts during Christmas break. Karen and I seemed to be the only two available to work any and all hours, both of us willing to sidestep church and whatever else we should have been doing.

Karen couldn't make it to church because of other obligations, although I had a feeling that she wanted to. I came to realize that, like me, she might have a lot to confess. I knew that for sure the first time I saw her stealing from the cash register.

Someone came in and bought three dozen donuts. She punched in the numbers, but I noticed they totaled only half of what the bill should have been. She put the customer's money in the register, took out the change, and pocketed half. The more I watched her, the more I realized that sometimes she didn't even ring up the sale and simply pocketed the whole bill. No one seemed to notice. Except me. Sometimes I felt as if I were the only one who noticed anything. Until the day Karen noticed me noticing her.

"You want in?" She smiled at me, her hand on her hip. "It's easy."

Karen enrolled me that Christmas break in her crash course on skimming, as she called it. And for several weeks following, she continued to school me on how to steal, which is what I was pretty sure it was called.

Those first few times, it didn't come easy. I dropped money on the floor. I couldn't remember how much I was really supposed to have charged and how much I really could take without getting caught. And every night when I got home, I felt so guilty. I knew it was wrong. It was s-t-e-a-l-i-n-g, no matter what Karen called it. But something about it—the excitement, the things I could buy with it, the school bills I could pay with it—had me hooked from day one.

I wish I could say that I had no idea it was wrong. Wish I could say that I did it only to help Papà with family bills or to save up for high school tuition. Wish I could say I did it out of fear or a sense of needing to belong. But I can't. Because while all of those reasons may have played a part, in truth, I did it, mostly, for me. And I became good—no, *great*—at it.

Even when Gunner came in during that Christmas-break week, I tested my growing skills. I snuck several dollars, always pushing the envelope, right under his nose. He never seemed to notice. Or maybe it didn't matter to him what I did. How bad I was. I was convincing myself he liked me for me, no matter how awful I might be.

It was a game I played, just as I was starting to realize that Gunner was playing one, too.

I wanted to confront him, at least ask him about his girlfriend comment. Had he gotten her a Christmas present? What was it? Had she gotten him a gift? What had she given him? Did he like it? I wanted to ask him what he expected me to say in response to his naughty-or-nice question. I wanted to talk to him, to tell him what was going on at home. I wanted him to "serve and protect" me and not anybody else.

But I said none of it. Too much risk of getting hurt.

I always liked to play out ahead of time the possible outcomes of whatever moves I made or things I said. While I had no idea how to play chess, I knew enough to know that winning was possible only when a player thought three moves ahead of any opponent. With Gunner, I never felt comfortable enough to play out certain scenarios, to think through what he might say or do, and what I would or should say or do in response. Thinking about it excited me as much as it scared me. And my fears always extinguished any smoldering fires.

Aurora wasn't afraid of anybody or anything. Most of all, she wasn't afraid of herself.

True, she was a lot older than I or even Gunner was, so she had a lot more experience. But watching her, I realized that it wasn't just age, because she was the same age as my own *mamma*, yet years apart from her in terms of sexuality, heat, and using it as power.

I found myself admiring her. I knew she played it up for tips, mostly. Much more than I or Karen ever did. I knew it was all for show. She probably never really did anything. Unless she wanted to. But I wondered how she controlled it, made sure she always stayed a step ahead of anybody who wanted to control her.

"Vaat can I get you? Me?" Aurora would joke with all the donut-eating boys and all the coffee-swigging men. She conceded to wearing the pink polka-dotted apron over those always cut-too-low tops and hemmed-too-high skirts. And often she wore pink stilettos to match. True, she had great legs. Always bare. Everybody loved them and said so. Even Gunner. And she'd hug and squeeze him tight to thank him. He'd flash her his signature smile in response.

It bothered me when he indulged her, and I knew he knew it.

In her embrace, over her shoulder, he'd give me a wink with one eye and raise his eyebrow on the other. It made me laugh. And feel special. At the same time, it made me feel something else: jealous.

Karen always restored order. And always played teacher.

"Now, you go on about your business. We sell donuts and coffee, nothin' more here. Ain't you got nobody to arrest?" she'd shout out, and everybody would laugh. Even the moms and dads who came in with their kids for after-church treats.

I would come home from the donut shop sometimes feeling defeated, jilted, not just by Gunner but by everything. Things were getting worse at home. Nothing seemed to matter. No one seemed to really care. Even school hadn't followed up. I knew they wouldn't. Nobody seemed to pay attention to anything.

"Cheer up, *POWwww*leeena. It's quittin' time!"

Papà was unable to come get me sometimes. It started out that he would ask me to see if I could find a ride home; then I'd ask Gunner, who always said yes; then I'd call home to tell Papà he didn't have to worry. It soon became the reverse: Gunner took me home with increasing frequency, to the point where I called Papà only if I needed a ride home.

I loved riding in his police car. Just Gunner and me.

He'd let me sit in the front, where Officer Brown usually sat. He'd turn down that police radio just low enough that he could still make out what they were saying but it wouldn't get in the way of our talking.

We had some great talks. He told me about some of the calls he had to respond to: drunk guys mouthing off, married couples fighting, school kids stealing, sometimes bigger-deal robberies or somebody snatching a purse or something from some lady at a bus stop.

I loved hearing his stories. I think he loved telling them to me.

I asked him once if he'd ever killed anybody. He said no. I told him I thought guns were cool. He said he thought so, too, adding that he liked the way they felt on his hip and in his hands. I told him my *papà* let me handle rifles when we went hunting together. I was a sure shot. But we hadn't gone for a while. I didn't tell Gunner why, and he didn't ask. Instead, he said maybe he would take me one day to shoot a gun like the one he carried.

I asked if I could hold it. We stopped at a red light, and even though he was saying he shouldn't, he pulled it out of its holster, made sure to tell me that the safety was on and not to point it anywhere but down at the floor, and handed it to me. Not up high—more like he slid it to me across my thighs. He kept his right hand there while his left hand steered. I took both my hands and put them on top of his, wrapping my fingers around either side to make sure I had the gun steady. Then Gunner slid his hand out, putting it back on the bottom of the steering wheel, moving his left arm so that it rested against the open window.

It was so warm out that night. The breeze coming in helped cool us off.

I did as Gunner said. I kept that gun pointed downward, my hands sort of having no choice but to be dragged down anyway; I didn't think a gun that size would feel so heavy. It seemed a lot heavier than even Papà's rifles. But it had been so long since I'd carried one on a hunting trip that maybe I'd just forgotten.

With one hand still holding Gunner's gun, I used my other to feel its smoothness, pretty much stroking it from end to end. I wondered what it would be like to actually point it at somebody, pull the trigger, and shoot. I was about to ask Gunner if he'd ever shot somebody—not killed them but hurt them—but before I could, he moved his left hand back onto the steering wheel and with his right hand motioned for me to raise the gun, tapping my thigh to put it back where we'd started.

He took my fingers and, starting from the tip of the gun, traced with me each part, naming as we went along. He didn't even take his eyes off the road; it was all by touch.

"This is called the barrel," he said. "And feel this raised part here?" He rolled my finger up and down the bump. "It's called the sight. You line that up with your target. You'll need to know that if you're gonna continue being a sure shot."

Gunner laughed and turned to wink at me.

I got a funny feeling all of a sudden—the jumblies, for sure, but something else. It always happened when he said something that made me realize that he listened to me, really heard what I was saying, I wasn't just some kid he was giving a ride home to. I felt warm inside. Not just because of how warm it was outside. And I couldn't look at him.

His hand stayed on mine. A few minutes later, his fingers wrapped themselves around the gun, sort of squeezing my thigh a little, as he picked up the gun and rested it in his own lap.

"We better put this away," he said. "I shouldn't even have let you play with it."

I just nodded.

I kept quiet about all the thoughts pinballing around in my head, some of which I understood and knew were normal, others that I wasn't so sure were.

Especially on Sundays, immediately after working at the donut shop, I'd arrive home, either courtesy of Gunner or with Papà, and everybody would be waiting for us. Sicilian Sunday dinners took place around 2:00 or 3:00 p.m., so by the time I got home, closer to four or four thirty or even five, everyone was beyond ready to eat. We always sat as a family, all six of us, at the kitchen table, every Sunday. House rules. We weren't allowed to miss.

One day, for a moment, I looked around the table and lulled myself into thinking how normal we all seemed.

For a moment.

But in the next, before I could get out of the way, red wine was dripping from the light fixture overhead, trailing its way, stark as blood, down our dingy off-white walls. The wine had splashed into my eyes, its sweetness instantly mixing with salty tears. It blinded me. I imagined this was what it must feel like for someone in a car crash with her head split open and blood dripping into her eyes, like what you sometimes see in the movies. As the haze of red began to fade, mockingly offering me a view of the world through rose-colored glasses, it was clear to me that, even with such visual aids, my world had become one drained of color.

Mamma had lunged toward Papà. Ironically, she was defending my brother. I'm not sure of exactly the what or the why, except that Ross had done something pretty stupid and somewhat serious enough to warrant Papà's smack to the back of his head. Mamma erupted, screeching that hitting on the head was not allowed. Papà told her to be quiet.

Ross choked back tears as he continued to shovel spoonfuls of whatever pasta we had been served into his mouth. Getting up from the table and trying to leave at that point would have been suicide—much safer just to pretend everything was normal. No clue what my other two sisters were doing. They often blended into the background.

Up to that point, I had not really witnessed my parents physically fighting. Sure, they shouted at each other; after all, it comes with being Sicilian, and in our case it was compounded by Mamma's illness. But raising a hand to each other? Never. To us? Yes. To each other? Never.

I had been told, however, that when Papà took Mamma to see her doctor, she would rage against him and throw things, like her purse, at him. But nothing that would cause bodily harm. And even though she threatened with knives and baseball bats, I had yet to see her use either one. That said, she was quite skilled in using her shoes as weapons. She had perfected her aim in such a way that even when we ran away from her, dashing around corners, those shoes seemed equipped with some sort of missile-accurate homing device. They always hit their intended targets. But that was us. Not him.

Mamma just kept coming at him. Screaming at him. Something about it being him, his fault, the reason for everything. She kept hitting, swiping at him, clearly wanting to hurt him. And nearly every one of her blows managed to make contact.

We four kids had gotten up from the table by now and moved to a safe distance away, but we were still positioned so that we could watch. I heard screams of "Stop it!" and "Please, don't," only to realize they were my own and my siblings'.

Having taken all he could, Papà finally grabbed Mamma's arms, crossing them in front of her while pushing her back against the wall. All the while, he kept saying, *"Basta!"*—begging her with pleas of "Enough!"—and then, with his final push, which really served to push himself off her, he told her to be careful, because he would kill her.

It didn't last long. And I don't remember where we all scattered to immediately following. Did we sit back down to finish our meals? Maybe. Did Mamma head up to her bedroom to cocoon herself in darkness under the covers? Probably. Did Papà escape to his garden out back, calming himself by concentrating on pulling the weeds that threatened to choke his prized produce? I'd bet on it.

The next day, Papà would leave for work, his face a web of red scratches courtesy of Mamma's claws. Papà would tell his colleagues at the factory, where he now worked second shift, that some hellish cat he had been trying to rescue had turned on him and attacked.

His explanation would not be so far from the truth.

He needed protection. We all did. We just didn't know enough to ask for it, or whom it was safe to ask.

Snow

We were trapped. Literally.

Nearly ten inches of snow descended upon us on New Year's Eve. I thought it was beautiful, at the start. I didn't even mind when Papà suited up in his warm hunting gear at midnight, taking his shotgun along and shooting it into the air outside the front of our home, a Sicilian tradition meant to ring in *buon anno*.

But the snow kept coming.

Two weeks later, the infamous Chicago blizzard of 1979 dumped another twenty inches or so of fresh snow. And by the end of that January, the streets, the sidewalks, the lawns, the rooftops—pretty much everything—became invisible, whited out under a record forty-seven-plus inches that would climb to more than eighty-eight before we saw even a hint of spring.

I wondered about that first flurry or two of individual snowflakes—so delicate, so airy, so weightless. I thought about how their accumulation could possibly create this. Roads impassable. Cars engulfed. Deadly accidents. Roofs caving in. People lost and even found frozen. Each tiny snowflake added upon another had the power to create an avalanche destined to kill whatever or whoever stood in its path. I wondered if each one realized how it contributed to the destruction.

For days, we went nowhere. Papà worried that he would lose his job at the factory if he didn't somehow figure out a way in to work. So he found one, some road clear enough to take him. He left hours earlier, got home hours later, and went straight to bed.

School had been shut down for days. Even the official high school placement test that was scheduled to be administered at St. Scholastic during the worst of the weather had to be postponed. I thanked God and the snow not only for conspiring to continue the delay of any questions related to what happened with Mamma during Christmas Day Mass but also for granting me a wish I couldn't help but make: asking God to find a way for me not to have to go to that all-girls school.

Ironically, that blizzard would end up sealing my fate, ensuring I *would* be sent to St. Scholastica, given that the paralyzing snow would move an entire city to oust the sitting mayor and replace him with Chicago's first and only female mayor, a woman named Jane Byrne. All it took was for Mamma, and especially Papà, to hear on the news for weeks how that lady-mayor wannabe just happened to be a graduate of St. Scholastica, and Mamma became more convinced that this was the place I was meant to be, while Papà inflated whatever aspirations he already had for me, pointing to the female politician on TV and telling me that's what I could be, if not more.

I smiled and nodded, but in my head I always ended his statement with *whether or not I want to be.*

We didn't talk about what had happened. The fight. Papà's slowly healing scratches a constant reminder. The dual threat now present, causing me to wonder who might end up killing whom first. Would Mamma bash Papà's head in with a baseball bat? Or would Papà choke the life out of her with his own bare hands?

We buried it, like everything else, under all that snow.

The snow broke official records that year on my birthday, February 12.

I don't remember that. I don't actually even remember turning fourteen. Maybe because officially, at least at the donut shop, I was turning seventeen. Maybe because I already felt at least twice that age, if not older. Maybe because it was too dangerous to tell anybody my age, given what it might lead to: possible questions about what turning sweet sixteen was like, for example. Which, obviously, I did not yet have a clue about.

I do remember bringing treats to my eighth-grade class.

I wished I could bring something like Angela's cupcakes, but Papà suggested something more from our heritage. I remember that at the same time, we were having some sort of international celebration at school, or at least a discussion about it in one of Mr. Jaminez's classes, so I figured I would have my birthday treat do double duty and decided on something very Sicilian and for sure unknown to my classmates.

I chose to bring horse meat.

Its official name is mortadella. It looks sort of like a bigger version of bologna, but with white polka-dot-looking things throughout it. Papà bought ours at a place down on Randolph Street—the real ethnic butcher's market. You had to know somebody to get in. It was the only place Papà was guaranteed that the mortadella was indeed made from horse meat—what he grew up with in Sicily, and not what the Americans had turned it into if purchased elsewhere: just another kind of pork-and-ham sausage.

Papà helped me with the presentation. We split the longest length of fresh Gonnella bread and, in between the tops and the bottoms, layered the mortadella alongside real provolone. Papà took a fork and raked it across the underside of the top piece of bread, then drizzled it with our best olive oil and generously sprinkled salt and pepper on it. He assembled the sandwich, wrapping it first in cellophane and then in aluminum foil, and sent me off to school with it.

I didn't tell my classmates we were eating horse meat. I told them only that it was a staple of our Sicilian diet, just like bologna was for them. I basically said, "Try it—you'll like it." They did. And they did—until I told them what the cold cut was made from.

I waited until they all had swallowed down their slice of sandwich.

I knew they would be too afraid to try it if they knew what it was at the start.

What I didn't know was how grossed out several students would be, some to the point of actually throwing up. What I didn't know was how much trouble I'd get in for "snowing" them, as a classmate named Mickey screamed at me. And what I didn't know—not for sure, until I *didn't* feel what maybe I should have felt—was how little I would care.

I thought them all to be babies—local yokels too young, too stupid, too inexperienced to understand anything. I thought about how easy and protected their lives must be. And I thought about how they'd never be able to be me.

I dismissed my classmates. Focused on my responsibilities. Home. School. Work. Home. Home. School. Work. Home. Just like a robot.

I tried to ignore Mamma's screaming of profanities in Italian and swearing she would murder us all as she sat up all night in the living room and we lay awake all night in our beds. Sleeping back then was a rare luxury, yet because of my A-plus grades, no one would have known it. I made sure of that. Mamma was convinced she saw a black wolf with yellow eyes each night at the window, snarling to get in. She pleaded in a frightening pitch for *il lupo/diavolo* to leave her alone. The shrill of her voice—sometimes enraged and sometimes so lost and alone—still haunts me to this day, when I let it.

I tried to be sure I was home more often than not. A sense of fear began to come over me. A fear of leaving my family alone. I felt so responsible. So old. I was in charge, and it was up to me to make sure they stayed safe. Especially my *papà*.

So I would rally the family, making sure we watched our favorites together on TV. Sunday nights: *All in the Family*; Monday nights: *Little House on the Prairie*; Tuesday nights: *Happy Days*, followed by *Laverne & Shirley*. Saturday nights, while I was at work, I made sure to remind them to watch *The Love Boat*, followed by *Fantasy Island*.

I usually sat on the sofa, arm in arm with Papà. Unless Mamma joined us. And when she did, her laser vision cut through me, accusing me, threatening me.

I often wondered why I had become the target. What had I done? When had I done it? When was the last time I had felt protected and safe and as if everything was normal?

As much as I cannot remember my fourteenth birthday, I could not forget my sixth. And that was maybe the start of it all.

"*Vedi, Paoletta, siamo lo stesso.*"

My Uncle Joe proclaimed it on our last joint birthday celebration, insisting that we were the same, despite the fact that he was born in 1905, was sixty years my senior almost to the day.

"Noooo . . . we're not the same." I burst into giggles.

Drawing our ages on a sheet of paper, he proved it. I was six, and he was "six-zero," and "zero counts for nothing." So, alas, we were the same!

I could not argue the point, nor did I want to.

Uncle Joe was Mamma's eldest brother. To us kids, he was like a grandpa, Santa Claus, and playmate all rolled up into one. He didn't have any children of his own, so he acted as if we were his. Sometimes I wished I were.

Uncle Joe had curly hair, just like mine. And he was tall, well over six feet. And skinny. And he walked with purpose on his long legs, one in front of the other, on a mission. Always. He never learned to drive, but that didn't stop him. He left our home daily to work in downtown Chicago, crafting custom home items like fireplaces, usually from marble. He took me to my first movie-theater experience—a double feature, *Chitty Chitty Bang Bang* and *Willy Wonka and the Chocolate Factory*—in the summer of '71. Whenever he came home, he always brought surprises, be they chocolate wooden shoes like the ones children from Holland wore, but tiny and much more tasty, or two live roosters, just in time for Easter, that we kept as pets in our basement, naming them Bonnie and Clyde. (We had no idea roosters were boys, obviously.)

Unfortunately, Bonnie and Clyde crowed at the crack of dawn, just like they were born to do. Papà didn't like all the noise, and so one morning, in the middle of their *cock-a-doodle-doo*-ing, we heard more of a *cockadurrrrrr* . . . Papà had strong hands and forearms, and he used them to strangle our pets. Even worse, that very night, Mamma roasted those roosters and served them up to us as dinner, a meal we were forced to eat despite our tearful refusals. We called Papà a murderer for days afterward.

Mamma didn't necessarily feel the same way about her oldest brother as we did about him. To her, Uncle Joe was bossy. It was difficult enough for her as a Sicilian wife to have four children and a husband to care for; she had grown tired of having to take direction from one more somebody, and, not knowing how to drive, she was pretty much a prisoner. So she wanted him out. One night, she told my father that he simply had to go. So my father told Uncle Joe that it was time he found his own place to live.

On the eve of the day he was to leave us, he ate his last meal with the family and turned in. We kids took our baths and dressed in our pajamas. And when we were all in the living room—all of us except Uncle Joe—he suddenly raced forth from his room, breathing hard, one hand held over his heart, eyes full of fear, shouting for us to call an ambulance.

He made his way back to his room, and Mamma followed. She eased him into bed as if he were a baby. I watched from the doorway. I watched her kneel at his bedside and cry. Uncle Joe turned his head and stared straight at me. Or more like straight through me. For the first time, he looked so old. And scary. Did he see me standing there? Did anybody else?

Then Uncle Joe threw up. Broccoli pasta—what we'd had for dinner. It was his favorite and one of mine. Now it was all over the bed and the floor and Mamma. She didn't seem to notice. She just kept screaming his name: "Joe. Joe!"

But he couldn't hear her anymore.

The ambulance came. They put Uncle Joe on a stretcher. We kids were shuffled out of the way. Papà tried to keep Mamma away, but she kept throwing herself on top of Uncle Joe, trying to shake him awake. We didn't know what to do, so we started skipping circles around the coffee table. My brother, Ross, and I locked eyes. I could tell from what I saw in his that this wasn't good.

Mamma was never the same after that. Nor were we.

At his funeral, Mamma dressed in black from head to toe. The hue of her skin, which looked more like the white of snow after it's been on the ground a couple of days, her pulled-back hair, and her lack of blood-red lipstick, which added to her ghostly appearance, frightened me. It was the first time I had seen her looking so deathly herself.

As I stood at my *papà*'s side, trying not to look at her, entertaining myself by tracing the swirly scrolls on the side of Uncle Joe's casket and examining the crisscross of metal holding it up, thinking how much it looked like one of those magician's boxes on TV that they used to cut a person in half, I was suddenly being hoisted overhead and hovered facedown over what no longer really looked like but was my Uncle Joe.

"*Dargli un bacio*," whispered my *papà*.

Give him a kiss?

Just a few days away from my seventh birthday, I reacted as any child of that age would have: I let out a screech, flailed my arms, squirmed my way out of my *papà*'s grasp, and in the process knocked over a tall, red, lantern-like candle holder placed at the head of the casket. Papà dropped me, and I plopped down on the carpeted floor, then scrambled to crawl out of the way while adults rushed in to right the fallen fixture before anything caught fire.

Kissing a loved one who had passed on the mouth was a Sicilian custom—one that I neither was prepared for nor wanted to do.

Curled up on the floor of the funeral home, watching the commotion I had caused, I connected with Mamma's eyes as they drifted to find me. Her look of disappointment, maybe even disgust, registered.

She slowly shook her head and flicked her wrist in my direction. I wanted to say I was sorry, I didn't mean it, but Mamma wasn't looking at me any longer. She had already shut me out, had lowered her head and was resting her forehead in the palm of her hand.

Slumped down into her chair, she started sobbing when it came time for them to remove his body from the church. She kept screaming, over and over, "*Ma, chi poteva sapere?*" and "*Non volevo cosi.*" And in between her asking out loud, "Who could have known?" and apologetically stating, "I didn't want it like this," Mamma just kept crying out Uncle Joe's name. The shrillness of it echoing off the walls caused me to shiver uncontrollably. And when she threw herself onto Uncle Joe, in his casket—she would have succeeded in literally climbing in had it others not held her back—I shut my eyes, covered my ears with my hands, and wished for Uncle Joe to please come back and make everything okay again.

If I had to choose one moment, one trigger, the start of Mamma's transformation, it would have to be the death of Uncle Joe. Her guilt, her silent suffering, her depression—all of it unchecked, unnoticed, untreated—led to where we were now. And for whatever reasons, whether she saw me as evil, promiscuous, competition, a threat, or maybe even a miniature version of herself whom she'd never much loved or could not forgive, I became her target, and in her states of paranoid delusions, that spelled trouble for me.

Uncle Joe's death seemed to be the catalyst for all things crazy. And was the moment when I lost my one adult guardian who made me feel special and safe and made everything seem normal.

Mamma had become convinced I was sleeping with my father and my brother. I was not. But that didn't matter.

One day, Ross was trying to teach me to dance disco to the Spinners' "Working My Way Back to You." I was fourteen and he was seventeen and we were in the basement downstairs. Mamma heard all the laughing and the music and slowly crept down the stairs to where we were. We both jumped when we realized she was just standing there, arms on her hips, a pose that loomed large, and a look on her face and in those cold, black, damning eyes that immediately caused Ross and me to freeze in place and just stare back at her. A moment later, realizing we were still holding hands, we dropped them to our sides.

Mamma advanced toward us. She silently turned off the record player. She kept her eyes on me. Ross scrambled away up the stairs, to somewhere. I turned to leave, too, but Mamma noticed purple eye shadow on my eyelids; Dahlia had lent me her makeup. It earned me a slap across the face of such force, it nearly knocked me down. I steadied myself, keeping the back of my head to her, my arms up as protection, and ran upstairs to the bathroom while she screamed, letting me know that only whores painted their faces, and I had better wash it off, and she had better never see me again doing whatever she was raging about my doing.

I shut the bathroom door behind me. Without a single show of emotion, I looked at myself looking back at me in the mirror and began to wash off any trace of color. I dared myself to cry.

Winter finally turned into spring.

I was graduating from eighth grade, and I had been chosen to sing the ceremony's duet with a classmate named Jake. His sister, Ellie, was our organist and music director. We practiced as much as possible after school at their home, not even a couple of blocks away from the school.

Ellie was a *mamma* herself, to a little boy named Nick. She was a lot younger than my *mamma*. And although we practiced singing and she made sure we did our homework, she also made sure each afternoon included some surprise. My favorite? A backyard impromptu roasting of marshmallows. But not just marshmallows.

Ellie showed me how to take two graham crackers, a Hershey bar, and melted marshmallows and make a sandwich out of them. She called them s'mores. I thought they were the best thing I had ever tasted in my life. She was surprised I had never heard of them before. "You don't know what s'mores are?"

I didn't know a lot of things other kids my age knew, and yet I knew so many more things that other kids my age did not.

I shook my head no. And said nothing more.

I had never heard John Denver's "Rhymes and Reasons" before. But I fell in love with the words, and the way Ellie's fingers danced across the organ's keys, and the sound of my voice singing harmony alongside Jake's, and the knowledge that I was finally getting out of grade school and growing up. And maybe soon getting myself away from so much craziness.

I wondered where I was going. I wondered about the rhyme and reason, just like the song did.

As I sang that duet in front of the entire congregation, with everyone applauding, not only did I feel like a star, but I knew God was speaking to me. I was hearing his message.

And I believed.

Shame

I didn't get the scholarship money. I didn't think I would. And
Papà paid the first quarter's tuition. I didn't think he could. The
school cost something like $1,700 a year, $425 payable every three
months. At least that's how much I remember I had to come up with
to keep me enrolled at St. Scholastica. I thought about what I would
buy with that money, if it were up to me. Guaranteed *not* to be on
the list was a nun-run education. But it didn't matter what I wanted.
It didn't matter that we could not afford the tuition. It didn't matter
that I really didn't want to be there. It didn't matter. Mamma was
immovable in her wanting me where I already was, and I was already
at St. Scholastica.

"Here" actually looked to me sort of like a prison from the outside, at least in the beginning. The building itself took up a couple
of blocks. And that didn't count the yard out back or the parking lot.
Dark reddish-brown bricks protected the exterior, and three iden-
tical floors, each showcasing white-trimmed, grid-like, nine-panel
windowpanes, at least a dozen standing guard side by side from one
end to the other, seemed to want to keep things in more than to let
anything out. Even the little hat-looking crow's nests—each with its
own set of prison-looking bars—that sat at the very top of each of the
grids, almost on the roof, looked to me like the very tops of castles,
the towers that kept princesses under lock and key.

I had traded in my blue-and-white grade-school jumper for a blue-and-white high school uniform. Same thing, really, just a bit different in the size of the plaid. I wore it with an institution-issued white button-down oxford and navy blue cardigan or pullover sweater. Knee-highs were white or navy, and shoes were the only thing left up to me to choose. And I did: saddle shoes I had bought with my own money, thinking I'd be unique, until I learned that pretty much every other girl was as unique as I was.

A curved one-way driveway let drivers drop off girls in front of double doors that led to a ground floor that housed mostly lab rooms, including the room where I learned to type on an Olivetti typewriter just like my Uncle Joe's, only these were electric and made of plastic and a lot easier to move and manipulate. I already knew how to two-finger-type, but this class taught how to type with all fingers at the same time and without looking. The teacher would time us, encouraging us to go faster and faster. I'd get lost in the speed of it, the race, and the sound of the pounding keys, almost all in thunderous unison, echoing off the concrete walls and downstairs corridor.

Up giant staircases that looked like sure-to-slip-on marble, hallways with rich wood wrapped their way around to homerooms and carpeted study halls and science labs and lockers and multistalled bathrooms. The school also housed an auditorium big enough to fit nearly 900 students, plus parents and friends, during various performances and ceremonies held each year, and its own chapel with watercolor-like frescoes of people, most of whom I had never heard of, painted with halos.

The school was attached to a monastery filled with cloistered nuns. I was never quite sure what they did all day, but rumor had it they were sworn to silence and prayer. I wondered what the penalty was for speaking. I wondered why God would give one of his creations a voice and then forbid the use of it.

I had never seen so many nuns before, especially the ones wearing full habits. They almost floated down the hallways, barely making a sound, not even showing whether they had feet. I wondered what they wore underneath those black robes. Did they have long underwear on in the winter? Did they wear nothing at all in the summer? Did they ever look at themselves without their clothes on? Was that a sin?

Each nun's face had me imagining not only her undergarments but also the color, length, and style of her hair. Maria from *The Sound of Music* had such an angelic face. When I first saw her twirl around, singing on that mountain, I thought she should have longer hair. But then I figured it just would have been too hot and bulky to keep long hair under that black veil with the white trim. I wondered if it was mandatory that all nuns cut their hair short, or if they had options. I wondered if any of them had her own Captain von Trapp, or maybe wished she did. I wondered if any of them could sing or wished she could.

Orientation at school included learning about our patron saint. Twin of St. Benedict, St. Scholastica formed her own version of her brother's monastery, except whereas his was just for males, hers would be devoted solely to females. Something about that made me wonder about her, made me think about what she thought of herself. She must have thought she was equal to her male counterparts. She must have thought she and other girls like her were worthy of exactly what the boys were getting.

Choosing to think that made me like her. And made me try to think just like her. I thought these all to be signs from God. I was meant to be here. I was good enough to be here.

"You dumb bunnies—can't you see this is a straight line?"

Sister Mary Michael brushed away her short-cropped, permed, gray-blond hair and held up her forefinger, gnarled and twisted from arthritis or something. She thought she was making a point, literally, while teaching us freshman geometry. But all she was really doing was making me and other girls in class laugh. Rather than get angry, however, Sister Mary Michael just looked at her own anything-but-straight finger, thought for a second about what she'd said, and started laughing herself.

"Oh, you know what I mean!" she said, turning her back on us and drawing more chalk triangles on the blackboard.

Sister Mary Michael was a nun—an old nun, maybe already in her fifties. But she must have been from some other, more modern order, because she dressed in street clothes: petite-size, neutral-toned, tweed-skirted suits. And she talked. Out loud, not just in prayer. Of course, often when she did, it was to tell us in her raspy voice that we were "dumb bunnies" who needed to sharpen our pencils and our minds or we weren't going to get anywhere in this life. But I didn't mind. I didn't take offense. I loved hearing her speak. I loved learning from her. She was smart and funny and warm. And she thought I had the smarts to move into her advanced class.

What I really hated was that we were called "Susies." *That* word made me feel more like a dumb bunny than the actual words "dumb bunnies." "SSA Susies." Hearing it made me cringe, and I was glad to know that even if I had wanted to and had the time to, joining some sort of sports team where some uniform would label me a Susie wouldn't be possible, given that the school and the girls just didn't have such structured sports; they had opted instead to buddy up with an all-male school, to have us girls watch and cheer them on, versus actually being the ones to play. The buddy system also held true for other extracurricular activities, like dances.

During study periods, the school offered us a TV room. Carpeted and cozy, it even had couches. I was one of the lucky ones to have free time for at least twenty minutes almost every day, right at the same time *General Hospital* aired. Luke, who loved Laura, and Laura, who was married to Scotty, were in a romantic triangle that kept us glued to the story line day after day. Dozens of girls crowded in, oohing and aahing breathlessly.

I wondered if the nuns had any idea what they were actually giving us access to.

Maybe they thought we'd all be watching Pope John Paul II, who visited Chicago during that October of 1979. Maybe some of us did. But most of us were watching something else.

We watched as Laura descended the stairs to the disco lounge Luke owned, the place where she worked. We heard her say that she had gone there looking for Scotty. But some were saying she had gone there "looking for it." Whatever her reasons, Luke was there. A little bit drunk. If I remember correctly, he was afraid for his life—some sort of mobster story line. Laura tried to help him. She refused to leave him. In the background, some pulsing instrumental played—Herb Alpert's "Rise." And Luke coaxed Laura into a dance. Even though she wanted to go. And the dance led to something more. Even though she said no.

It was a TV first.

And no one was quite sure what "it" was. Seduction? Rape?

Everyone seemed to be talking about it. And most of the girls had opinions. Loud ones. Arguing over "it."

I had feelings about it. Confused feelings. But I kept them to myself.

I made my way to and from home-school-work-work-home-school on the public transportation system. The stop was only about three blocks from the school, about the same from home, and about the same from the donut shop. *Three, three, three, just like the Holy Trinity*, I thought.

Ever since school had started, in late August, Joel had been the driver of the bus that took me home. Sometimes he even drove the morning bus that took me to school. I wondered what kind of hours he kept, given that sometimes, in the very same day, he escorted me in both the a.m. and the p.m. But I never asked. Or if I did, I've forgotten the answer.

Joel and I became fast friends. He was nice. And cute. He looked younger than Gunner but was still at least twice my age. Maybe mid-thirties. He had bushy brown hair and a scruffy beard. After our first couple of weeks together, he always made sure whenever I was on his route to wait until I crossed the street before he took off. He said he wanted to make sure I got home safely. After the first month or so, he always insisted I sit up front with him. The route was full of rough characters. Or so he said. After the first couple months, around Halloween or so, he insisted I sit either directly behind him or in the first seat to the side. He didn't care that those seats were reserved for old people and people with disabilities. At that time, neither did I.

The Halloween prior, I had snuck in to see the movie *Halloween*. Jamie Lee Curtis played a teenager living in a house that fifteen years earlier had belonged to a family that included a boy who stabbed his older sister to death. Having been diagnosed as a head case, the boy was locked away in a mental institution. He escaped and on Halloween night returned to revisit his murderous spree on unsuspecting Jamie. Ironically, Cathy drove me to see the movie. It was my kind of film. I loved horror flicks. The scarier the better. Not so much Cathy. Or maybe it had to do with the older sister being murdered. Maybe the whole thing hit too close to home for her. I don't know.

I loved to be scared. In the movies, at least.

The kind of scare I was living with at home, however, wasn't as much fun.

Mamma had the habit of appearing behind dark corners in our house, especially as I was trying to leave the premises for school, when the night sky had yet to give way to any sign of light. She would pop out from the shadows and grab me by the arm and beg me not to go. She would tell me that if I did, bad things would happen to me. Bad things that I would orchestrate. Bad me. Bad seed. Bad, bad, bad. Words cannot describe the fear instilled in my child self each and every morning—mornings that came following nights filled with screams of imagined torture and threats and sleepless suspense of whether or not you or someone you loved would even be alive when dawn broke.

I always expected the unexpected, whether she scared me before I headed out to school or was waiting for me on the other side of some door when I got home from wherever I had been. Still, on some days, she'd be nowhere to be found. Until we found her. Either sitting zombie-like in her sewing room or sleeping under the covers in her bed. Just like in a horror flick, inside my head I'd hear my own voice screaming, *Don't go in there!* and yet I would, and sometimes it'd be okay, sometimes not. I just never knew.

The only difference between the movies and real life for me was that the former didn't faze me, while the latter seriously freaked me out. But nobody would have known. Outwardly, I pretty much reacted the same, making sure that to the casual observer, nothing appeared to be less than normal.

I guess I was better at it than I thought, masking my true feelings from others. Sometimes I even masked them from myself. And sometimes I wasn't sure what I was putting out or what others were even seeing. As good at it as I thought I was, I was starting to wonder if, in reality, maybe I really just sucked at it.

Gunner had told me he loved Fleetwood Mac. I had no idea who he was. He wasn't my Styx, but I would learn that "he" was a group, and that Stevie Nicks was a girl—sexy, raspy—and I would learn all the words and belt out their tunes whenever the radio at the donut shop played Gunner's favorite, "Dreams."

I wanted to thank him for being my friend. His fortieth birthday was coming up. I knew this because for days prior, Gunner kept telling me he wanted "something special." Part of me knew I could afford *Tusk*, the new Fleetwood Mac album that had just come out. I thought I might surprise him with that as a gift. But then part of me—whatever part of me remained that still knew right from wrong, truth from lies, good from bad—began to panic. Something inside me knew. I was no dumb bunny. I knew what Gunner meant when he said "something special." And it wasn't a "today's special" donut.

For days, I agonized. I went to some gift shop for platonic inspiration. I found a card that happened to have a donut on its front side. A big, fat, sugary, jelly-filled donut. The words said, "Turning 40 is like a jelly donut . . ." I flipped open the card to see the image of the donut, now half-eaten, with jelly oozing out, crumbs littered about: "The best part is in the middle."

Perfect. Divine intervention. No matter how bad or "not normal" a girl I was, I just knew this card and its message was a sign from God. He had not abandoned me. And this message would surely set things back on a less jumbly path with Gunner.

I looked around and slipped the card into my jacket. Waving good-bye to the clerk, I exited with my stolen prize. Stealing had now become common practice for me. It didn't matter if I had the money to buy. Why bother? Nobody seemed to notice. It didn't seem to matter. Not much did.

I found a birthday candle in some old drawer at home. And I hatched my innocent plan. Gunner's birthday was on my next scheduled night at work. I'd tell him I had "something special" for him. I'd make him my own "today's special" donut. I'd put a candle in a strawberry-jelly double-filled donut, light it, sing him "Happy Birthday," and give him the card, and that'd be the end of it.

Even I did not believe me. Or maybe I did.

Gunner bounded into the shop.

"You been practicing?" he sang out.

"Practicing what? Singing you 'Happy Birthday'?" I replied, all sassy.

He immediately stepped behind the counter.

It was a night. I was working solo. We were alone.

The jumblies were back. But this time, I was genuinely afraid.

"Help me solve my pussy problem?" He started to pull the tape from the dispenser.

Tell him. Tell him now. Tell him that the best part is in the middle, sort of like middle age and his life. Tell him, my inner voice screamed at me.

"Wait!" I said. "Your present . . ." I gave him his card. He laid out the strips of tape along the counter. Dozens of them. He took the card from me and started to open it.

"Wait!" I said again. "Wait." I slipped into the back room, where I had already set out my big, fat, jelly-filled surprise. I plunked the candle inside. I lit it and walked back out to the front counter, where Gunner had torn the envelope open and was reading my card. I started to sing.

"Happy birthday to you. Happy birthday to you. Happy birthday, dear Gun . . ." I trailed off.

Silence.

"I told you you should try our strawberry-filled donuts." I said it so softly, I wondered if I really had said it out loud.

Gunner read the card aloud, his tone mocking.

"Best part is in the middle." He blew out the candle, took the donut from my hands, and ate it almost in its entirety in one giant bite. Strawberry jelly exploded around his lips. A bit plopped onto his uniform. He grabbed a napkin.

I felt frozen.

"I hope tape lifts up cat hair *and* jelly." He smiled when he said it. But it wasn't a smile. It was something different.

Gunner took my hands and wrapped them in the sticky-side-up tape.

At that moment, I knew what "it" was, and that it was happening. Or maybe I didn't know. Not fully. But I was sure almost all the parts of me knew.

And I knew it wasn't what I wanted.

I pulled my hands, slowly, back toward me.

He wouldn't allow it. He finished the taping. Pressed them to his chest.

I said nothing, not knowing what to say. Wondering why he was even forcing me to have to say it.

"You're wise. Beyond your years." He stroked his torso with my taped-up hands, dragging them like a lazy lint brush that kept getting stuck in spots. He pulled me closer to him, pushing me into the back room.

"Gunner, I need to be out here," I said, tears unexpectedly welling up in my eyes.

This is my friend, I thought. *Almost like my father. I don't want this.*

"Hey, you know me," he cooed.

But I realized that the Gunner who was in front of me was someone I did not know. Or maybe he was the same Gunner I should have known but didn't. Or maybe I was not me. Didn't know me. Or maybe I no longer knew what or whom I did or didn't know.

He eased me against the stainless-steel table where the bakers rolled out dough. I kept pulling myself toward me and away from him, but it was as if he were stuck to me. He kept advancing. I kept retreating, until I could not back up any farther.

"Gunner, I need to be out there."

"Shhhhh . . ."

He held the back of my head with one hand and bruised my lips with his, shoving his tongue into my mouth. I had never tasted tongue before. I did not like it. Even if I could still taste strawberry. When he bent my body backward, I started to cry. I could feel the tears running down my cheeks. I thought about how I would explain the flour stains on the back of my uniform.

Wait! The word hammered the inside of my head. *WAIT!*

But all that came out was a squeak of the word "no" as Gunner took his hand and covered my mouth. I could not speak, but I could still see him. He could see me.

My eyes screamed at him. *Look at me. Look at me, please. It's me.* I knew he saw me. But he was not seeing. Not listening. Or maybe he was, and that's why he moved his hand to partially cover even my eyes.

Still I could see him.

And then I really saw him; I recognized his face. The face my mother said I made when doing what I should not have been doing, touching myself down there.

I watched as if I were watching someone else. As if I weren't there.

His other hand was now under my skirt, inside my panties. Touching me. But I did not feel the way I did when I touched myself. I saw it in his eyes: he registered surprise. I am not sure if I knew back then what the reason for his look might have been, but, thinking back, I know it was because I was dry. And he must have expected me to be wet.

His eyes met mine. They registered disgust. And when he took his hand out of me and lifted it to his lips and slathered his fingers with his spit—just like he licked them when he was finished eating his strawberry-iced donuts—I relaxed my body. On purpose. Not for pleasure, but because it hurt too much not to.

I looked away. His other hand still pushed against my mouth, my nose, making it hard to breathe. But with my head a bit to the side, it was easier. I scanned the room and took inventory of the things that I had come to know. Maybe I was checking to make sure I wasn't as wrong about them as, obviously, I had been about Gunner, or about myself: phone, didn't dial out; jelly and cream dispensers, where I'd double-filled his birthday present earlier that day.

Oh God. Something was in me. Maybe it was just his saliva fingers, but it hurt; it felt like his whole fist. Or maybe it was something else. His face. *Don't look at his face.* I saw flashes of my mother making fun of me. Donut racks. French crullers cooling. I loved French crullers. My mind wandered. *I must really be what my mother says I am. Otherwise, how could this be happening? Why doesn't anybody help me?*

And then a familiar sound reached my ears. I heard the angel bells. Someone had come into the donut shop. Someone who had no idea what was happening in the back room had come into the donut shop. *I'm here. I'm here. Please come here.*

With my mouth to the side, a bit askew from his grip, I managed to get out, "I have a customer. I have to go. Someone's here. Gunner. I have to go."

Gunner took a moment before releasing me. He looked confused. As if he had no idea where we were or what was going on. He loosened his grip on me.

We looked at each other. I wiped away my tears. I silently soothed myself: *Everything is normal. It's normal. It's okay. I'm okay.*

Gunner shook his head like a dog ridding itself of unwanted water or sweat. I straightened up. My back was killing me. I adjusted my panties and my uniform, and I escaped.

I walked toward my unsuspecting savior. "May I help you?" I smiled a fake smile, having no idea what I really looked like. Did this angel know? Did he see it in me? It didn't seem to matter to him. He ordered a dozen donuts. He was oblivious to what had just happened.

What *had* just happened?

Gunner, undetected, breezed out of the back room, brushed by the man, and exited.

The angel was speaking to me. I tried to focus. "I said six of those 'today's specials,' and the other half dozen any kind you choose."

I folded a box and began filling the angel's order.

Surrender

This wasn't how it was supposed to be.

This wasn't like Rocky in his wifebeater undershirt cornering Adrian in his apartment.

I thought about it. Played the scene out in my head again. Adrian kept backing up. I had never noticed that before. Was she afraid?

Rocky had taken Adrian. And she was changed afterward. Completely. For the better.

But then it came to me. I realized at that moment that that wasn't how it always worked. Being taken. And being better. I felt horribly worse at that moment in my life than I had ever felt before.

And the voices battled.

How could he have done that to you?

How could you have let that happen?

Was it me?

How could it not be?

Please, God. It can't be me.

Where was Papà? Why had he not yet come for me?

I waited. I watched. I couldn't stop my thoughts.

When he did arrive, would I—should I—tell him?

What would I tell him?

This wasn't how it was supposed to be. I hated how I felt. Inside me. About me. Was it like Mamma said: I had made it happen; I was to blame?

This can't be me. Please, God, not me.

I could not form the words.

What if I told my father?

Gunner was my friend. I had made him a special donut. I had lit that candle. *Happy birthday to you. Happy birthday . . .*

Best part in the middle.

He shouldn't have put his hand there. On my mouth. Covering my eyes. That wasn't how it was supposed to be. Rocky didn't do that. It was supposed to be different.

Rape.

The word wormed its way into my mind, then wrapped itself around my heart.

RAPE.

Squeezing it.

R-A-P-E.

It couldn't be.

Such an ugly word. A four-letter word.

Not like L-O-V-E.

I shut my eyes. Trying to keep from crying. But I could not stop the tears. I made my way around the front of the shop, around the snakelike counter, and into the bathroom. I shut the door behind me. In the filthy room, no bigger than a closet, I wanted to turn on the lights. I wanted to look at myself looking back at me in the mirror.

I did neither.

I just stood in the darkness.

If I told Papà, if I said that word, what would happen as a result?

If he confronted Gunner, Papà's rage might get the best of him. And Gunner, being the law, would have the ability to silence Papà in some form or fashion forever.

But what if I told Papà and he did nothing? What if, after I told him, he saw in me what Mamma did? What if this proved her right? What if he didn't believe me?

What did I even believe?

If Papà did nothing, I would lose the one adult in whom I still believed.

And *that* would be the end of me. *That* would send me to a place deep inside me that I feared festered, and that for now I was successful at keeping at bay. I worried that *that* place, that thing that secretly conspired to demonize me, awaited patiently its chance to fully own me. Would this do it? Send me over the edge? Would this be *my* trigger? Would this make me like Mamma? If Papà knowingly chose to do nothing on my behalf, would the evil that obviously was within me finally be unleashed?

"Well, POWwwwleeena, this is the best donut ever created. Mmm. This is so good."

Shut up. Shut up. I wish I had never told you my name.

I couldn't get Gunner's face out of my mind. His voice.

I needed to tell. Someone. My *papà*. I needed him to understand. To call me his "baby girl." I wanted him to kill Gunner. Erase him. From me. From this place. From ever having touched me. My heart. I did not care at that moment if it meant Papà would go to jail for murder. Gunner deserved to die. And I wanted Papà to do it. I did not care about the consequences.

The angel bells tinkled.

I shook myself to the present, wiped my tears and washed my face with cold water, then exited the bathroom. Papà had entered the donut shop. Looking so old and fatigued, but smiling for my benefit, he sat on the pink stool that had become reserved for Gunner.

I wanted to run to him. To cry. To tell him.

"How my baby girl?"

I half smiled in response. He didn't notice. But I noticed that his words to me somehow sounded different.

I made my way behind the counter. I poured him a cup of coffee. At that moment, it dawned on me that while I knew how Gunner took his coffee—black with two sugars—for all the times my father had sat with me, for all the times I had served him a drink, I had to keep asking how he liked it. The realization at that moment stunned me. What did that say about me?

"*Paola,*" Papà began, before I could say anything. "*Mamma non sta bene.*"

"I know, Papà. I know that Mamma is sick."

Papà swallowed back his tears. I looked at him. I thought my eyes were searing his. I wanted to scream at him: *Look at me. Look at me! Don't you see anything? Don't you see what just happened to your baby girl?*

I stayed silent. I let him finish.

Papà then asked. As if it were nothing.

He asked me to ask Gunner to help us.

My mind struggled to understand his words. He said that Mamma believed the police needed to be called in. She said she wanted to tell them about our conspiracy to kill her. The computers we had planted throughout the home to monitor her. The murderous plots we had against her. So Papà had an idea. He figured we would get Mamma the police protection she desired and, in doing so, gain her trust enough that the cops could do the dirty work of having her committed. Once Mamma was in a hospital that specialized in her illness, we would finally be on the road to recovery. Or so Papà reasoned.

I stared at him. And I thought about the guy my father was asking me to ask for help. The guy whose job it was to serve and protect.

"No."

The word just popped out of my mouth.

"*Ma perche 'no'?*"

I tried to explain, to answer his question of "Why not?" but the words would not come. I could not look into my *papà*'s eyes, the ones that were all glassy and clearly telling me that this was our last possible solution, and tell him the truth. I didn't even know what the truth was. Not for certain. And I simply could not take from him what I realized was his last hope.

I asked him to please not make me do this, barely whispering it.

He again asked why, reiterating that Gunner was our friend. Telling me that Gunner loved me. He protected me. He would help us. He was our only chance.

I fumbled with words like "embarrassing" and "crazy" and "others knowing."

And then I once again gave in to something I did not want. I reluctantly agreed to do as my *papà* asked.

I would ask Gunner—my friend, my protector, my rapist—for help.

I called in sick that next day. I didn't tell Mamma or Papà. I pretended to still go to work. I was getting a ride, I said. No need to take me. Nobody asked with whom.

I didn't want to be at the donut shop. I couldn't. But I didn't want to be at home, either.

I didn't sleep well, if at all, that night. My thoughts wouldn't shut up long enough to let me. And one voice in particular refused to cease its constant refrain, no matter what else I said.

It's your fault. You know that, right?

I didn't want this. Not like this.

You got exactly what you wanted.

This isn't—

It is. Your fault. You asked for it. Your fault. You asked for it. Your fault.

Even when I stopped arguing, the voice still wouldn't stop saying it.

I knew I needed to tell. Someone. Anyone. I knew I needed just one somebody to listen. To hear me. To tell me I wasn't to blame.

I walked to church. God would listen. He would say I was okay.

But He didn't. Instead, what I got was eternal damnation.

"Promise me you'll come to church on Sunday, or I will not absolve you of your sins."

I did not stay for Mass. I walked out.

"I cannot absolve you of your sins."

The words Father Tierney had spoken kept echoing through me. My sins. Mine.

I could not tell Papà. And the Church would not hear my confession. And I knew that without absolution, I was headed for hell. The Bible was clear. I didn't have to look it up to be sure; it was one of Mr. Jaminez's favorite verses, Matthew 16: 18–19: *Now I say to you that you are Peter, and upon this rock I shall build my church, the Kingdom of Heaven. Whatsoever thou shalt bind on Earth shall be bound in heaven: and whatsoever thou shalt loose on Earth shall be loosed in heaven.*

Good thing I no longer cared—or at least, that's what I tried to convince myself of.

I felt taken. As in, tricked. Because I had trusted. Gunner. The Church. God. Papà. Myself.

I meandered through the maze of parked cars in the lot, making my way to the sidewalk and continuing to where, I did not know. I couldn't go back home until at least a little bit closer to my normal quitting time.

I crossed in front of Ellie's house. I thought about knocking on her door. Telling her. I'm not sure why I thought she'd listen, but I did. She'd say I was okay. She'd tell me what to do.

I didn't, though.

I crossed the street and then found myself in front of my friend Jenny's house. I thought about stopping, maybe not to tell her, but just to spend some time there. Her mom and dad were so nice. They would listen. Maybe I would tell them.

But I didn't do that, either.

I don't know what I ended up doing, where I ended up going. I remember going into the grocery store and then the drugstore nearby. But that's about it. My guess is, I probably stole some stuff.

I remember the walk home, making sure to stick to secondary streets, just in case Papà might be driving around and see me.

I walked along the railroad tracks. That was the route that Cathy, Ross, and I took every morning and every afternoon going to and from grade school when we had just started at St. Peter's. I was in third grade, Ross in fifth, Cathy in eighth. That was where we, one sunny day, found a brown-papered package just sitting off to the side. We tore into it, just enough to see what it was. We had never seen a dirty magazine before, or at least I hadn't yet. Issue after issue, I don't know how many in all, of virgin *Playboy* magazines peeked back at us.

Ross was elated. Cathy and I were curious.

We hid them in our book bags and together carried them all home. In Ross' room, we sat on the floor, each of us checking out the different magazines, voting for our favorite cover girls, choosing favorite poses, picking out best body parts, saying things like, "I'd never do that" (Cathy and me) or "Wow!" over and over again (Ross).

It all seemed so long ago. So innocent.

When Ross told us he would "take care of them," I just assumed he would throw them away. He did, in a way, but not before tearing out all of his favorite pages, none of which was an article, and hiding his girls under his mattress.

Mamma, who came across his stash while changing the sheets, tore after him with shoe in hand. The sight of Ross, his arms full of now-squashed-up pictures, flying down those stairs had made me laugh out loud.

Now it made me think of how gullible I had been. And it made me wonder if it played any part in the fact that Mamma, just a few years later, had begun keeping knives and baseball bats under her mattress and believing she saw herself naked in published magazines.

I made it home a couple of hours earlier than expected. I expected lots of questions about why, but Papà wasn't around, Mamma was in bed, and nobody asked anything. So I didn't offer up any explanations.

I had a few more months to go until I turned fifteen. I had to wait almost the entire winter season. No longer a child—at least not one who believed in Santa, the Tooth Fairy, the Easter Bunny, White Hats winning, Happily Ever After, or the existence of Officer Friendly—but not really a woman, either. Nor very sure that I even wanted to be one.

When I returned to the donut shop, I didn't see Gunner for a while. A long while. He just didn't come in anymore.

And I cared that he didn't.

Officer Brown would walk in, always asking for two coffees and two donuts, one of those always being the strawberry-iceds that Gunner loved to devour. I knew Gunner must be waiting out in the squad car, the motor running, like some sort of accomplice to a crime in charge of driving the getaway vehicle. I always made sure that I was the one to wait on Officer Brown. Jerome. James. I always made sure to stare through to the backs of his black eyes. But I never could tell for sure if he knew that his partner was a rapist. Or if in their locker room or in their squad car, Gunner had told him how he'd gotten it on with the PYT at the donut place. Or if he knew nothing at all.

When Officer Brown smiled at me, even though it was the same smile, I wondered if he knew.

I wondered if everyone knew, because from that moment on I seemed to be "fair game." Even to my regular customer, Ron. He came in late one night. As usual, I had his standing order at the ready. He sat in his usual seat. I took my place, as usual, on the other side of the counter, leaning on my right elbow, handing him his dunker donut and chatting with him about something benign, when suddenly Ron took my arm and started stroking it. Stroking me. Up and down, up and down. His wrinkly, leathery fingers caressed my baby-soft upper arm. It took me a moment for it to register. A second later, I recoiled. Disgusted.

It was as if some all-points bulletin had gone out about me.

I tried to ignore, to pretend, to keep on performing, as everyone else expected me to, regardless of who they were. I learned not to share or ask for help. I learned to survive solo. Any feelings I had, I stuffed down and silenced. Alone at night in the donut shop, I played my music—like Supertramp—in the background, "The Logical Song" speaking to me.

Illogical me always wondered when next he'd come visit. As much as I wished he would, I prayed he wouldn't. Things still hurt. Especially the pain in my chest, which made me feel as if my insides were caving in on themselves.

And so I ate.

Almost unconsciously, I began soothing myself silent, stuffing myself with jelly and frosting—that sickly-sweet, sticky strawberry that Gunner loved so much. Hidden from view in the back room, supposedly filling and frosting the freshly baked yeast and cake donuts that sat row upon row on the racks that watched it happen, I played a game with myself. For every one I filled or frosted, I took a shot of strawberry jelly, strawberry cream, or strawberry frosting, straight into my mouth from the machine's spout, or immersed my fingers in gooey goodness and licked them clean one by one, mimicking—and thinking—all things Gunner.

It was the start of my weight problem. Just the start. But nobody noticed. Not even me, I think. It just wasn't a big enough deal to worry about when it was stacked against everyone and everything else demanding priority status.

Papà kept asking when I would ask Gunner for help. I dragged my feet until I could stall no longer. Mamma had become out of control, going to neighbors' homes, whether she knew them or not, and telling them to let her know whether naked photos of her appeared in magazines. Telling them that if she were to die suddenly, we were the ones who would have done it.

On this particular winter day, Styx had a new single topping the charts: "Babe." It played over and over again on the radio. I prayed it was another message from God, assuring me of how Gunner really felt about me. But the voices insisted I was a fool.

Officer Brown had come in for his usual and was about to step back outside. The tinkle of the angel bells attached to the top of the doorway had already started to chime. A blast of cold air blew in, slapping me across my face. It woke me up.

Papà had begged me to ask Gunner for his help in committing Mamma. I could stall no longer. I *had* to ask.

"Hey, Officer Brown . . ."

Brown paused and turned to look at me. The words got caught a bit in my throat. I had to swallow a few times to say it out loud. But I did.

"Tell Gunner I miss not seeing him. Ask him to stop in. Soon. I need to talk to him."

Brown nodded. A brief dusting of concern swept his face. He exited.

And I hated myself for asking. Hated myself for wanting. For needing—and, of all people, him. I could not accept how little I must have meant to him. He had taken what he wanted. And he had abandoned me. He had thrown me away. At fourteen, I could think only that he wasn't the Rocky Balboa to my Adrian. He wasn't feeling what Styx sang about in "Babe." I was nothing more to him than the flavor of the month, the latest sweet to be had for free.

It wasn't just about the betrayal of who he was and what he did; it was more so that after the fact, he no longer wanted me.

On the day I made the ask, it wasn't an ask. Rage had begun to fester within me. I knew I was as angry at Gunner for continuing to show up at the donut shop only when he felt like it, which was almost never, as I was at him for not showing up as often as he used to. To talk to me. Keep me company. Be my friend.

Something else was happening, too. I was starting to realize that I was the one in charge. Even the fact that he no longer came in solo, but rather always with Officer Brown at his side, showed me that Gunner was afraid. Of me. And I was glad.

The angel bells rang. Officer Brown and Gunner entered. I motioned Gunner to the side. Far, far away from where it happened.

I could not really look at him as I said it: "Gunner, I'm in trouble."

But the silence that followed caused me to look up and directly at him. Those ice-blue eyes. That mouth, no longer smiling brightly but tightly drawn into a thin line.

I will never forget his face or the words that came from him. Barely audible, he leaned low and seemed to spit out into my ear, in a continuous string of words, as if he had been waiting for the question and preparing his response, "You're-pregnant-*no*-way-can-it-be-mine-I-never . . ."

My body instinctively pulled back, not hearing the rest of what he was saying. I suddenly could not catch my breath. I had thought I had prepared myself. I had thought I was in control. But his words hollowed me out from my core. I felt like I was about to throw up. His words wounded, accused.

And yet the girl in me wished for and wondered what the response would have been had this been Rocky talking to Adrian.

I so wished I had never opened my mouth to him. I so wished I had never, ever started talking to him. And I so wished I had never let my heart believe in him.

I shook my head, whimpered out the word "no," and swallowed my tears. I met his stare and matter-of-factly explained what Papà wanted to have happen. The look in Gunner's eyes when I told him what was going on at my home, with my *mamma*, was one of disbelief mixed with shame.

I took pleasure in it. I renewed my steely exterior self. And at that moment, I knew I had him. I had the power. I *was* in control. He owed me now. And he was on board to deliver.

I don't remember how we orchestrated it. I don't recall if Papà met with Gunner and me at the donut shop some Friday night to hatch our plan to capture and put away my *mamma*. I can't seem even to imagine what those conversations must have been like. But I know they had to have happened.

I know because one night, Gunner and his official squad car appeared at our home, the lights flashing behind him as he knocked on our door. I remember his eyes, avoiding my gaze. And I remember how I refused to take my eyes off his.

Gunner played his part beautifully. He told Mamma that they were investigating her claims and she needed to come with him.

Gunner's words worked.

My mother believed and was taken.

I no longer did, and I promised myself I never would again. Believe or be taken.

Slush

I think we ended up putting her in the University of Chicago hospital that time, but I can't be sure—there were so many hospitals. What I do know is that wherever we placed Mamma, whatever hospital we tricked her into, we were not allowed to visit for a couple of weeks.

Hospital rules. The psych ward demanded it.

And I could not have been more thankful. My entire family, for the first time in I don't know how long, slept. The house was silent, the tension, fear, drama—all of it—nonexistent. And even though we all knew it was just for a few weeks, we rejoiced in it, welcomed it, pretended it would go on forever like normal.

Papà kept asking me to thank Gunner again for helping us. I wanted to thank him, too. But I didn't do either. Mostly because I rarely, if ever, saw him.

On the day we were allowed to visit Mamma in the hospital, we all dreaded it. Okay, maybe not all of us. Maybe not Papà. Maybe he still held out hope. Maybe not my siblings. I really don't know. But me? I could have left her there to rot. The thought of interrupting silence and normalcy—purposely—to go get a dose of noisy crazy was not on my list of things to do. Ignorance was so bliss. And I needed not to know what was going on with Mamma, at least until I had more of a handle on what was going on with me.

We ate dinner at home. Already it was dark outside, and cold. Slush and stale snow on the ground. Trees barren, skeletal. We put on our coats and piled into the car. I remember sitting in the backseat, by the left window. I paid little attention to what was being said in the car or even to where we were going. I fully expected Papà to ask me what I was thinking, but he didn't. I could see, though, that he wanted to. I could see his eyes trying to speak to me from the rearview mirror; I pretended not to notice.

Papà was like a human GPS. He could navigate us through anything to anywhere. I was not worried about not getting to our destination. Just the opposite.

We parked the car. Inside, outside? No memory of where. We entered the hospital doors. The lobby was like every other lobby we had been in before. The nice lady at the front desk checked us in. All five of us were allowed to go up to the psych ward where Mamma was kept under lock and key, but once up there, the lady explained, we'd be allowed in only two at a time. I silently decided I wanted to go last. If at all.

Like a robot, I followed my family. We walked down long halls, void of anything memorable. Just a flood of light, similar to walking down death row in prison, I guessed. We jammed into an elevator. Maybe we saw other people, doctors or nurses, maybe, but I remember only us. Alone. All together.

We reached the nurses' station of the floor Mamma was on. I remember somebody saying something about Mamma's taking some cooking classes and making friends.

What? As much as I wasn't really paying attention, that comment snapped me to attention. In my own head, I was certain they must be talking about somebody else. Or they, too, must be crazy. *My mamma? This* version of Mamma? Not possible.

But I said nothing. Nobody listened anyway.

Mamma was in a tiny, two-person-but-really-big-enough-for-just-one-person room. The other lady who shared her living quarters was invisible to me. I'm sure she was somebody else's mom or sister or daughter or . . . who cared? I found it difficult to conjure up any caring for the woman who belonged to me, let alone for anyone else.

I remember seeing Mamma for the briefest of moments. I think my brother and I were the first duo told to go in and see her. For some reason, I was sent out of the room to get something. What it was or why, I don't remember. Ross was left alone with Mamma. I do remember that just before I exited the room, she had her little suitcase in hand and was saying good-bye quite cheerfully to her roomie. I didn't put two and two together.

Next thing I knew, Mamma was missing. No trace of her anywhere in the hospital. It was like she had just vanished. Papà was bewildered. We kids were confused. The doctors and nurses on the floor raced around, apologized, expressed complete disbelief that anybody could slip out of their psych ward, let alone the entire hospital, undetected.

They had no idea whom they were dealing with. But I knew.

It dawned on me that the cooking classes and making friends were all just an act—part of a calculated, well-thought-out plan. Her plan. Just as we had concocted ours to get her in there. And dread enveloped me, in anticipation of what I was sure lay in wait for us as a result.

We were assured that the authorities had been called and that they would comb the city, looking for Mamma. They would find her and bring her back, they promised.

Keep her, I thought.

We all walked without a word back to the car. We all took our same places. Papà started to drive off, winding his way up and down the streets surrounding the hospital, asking us all to keep an eye out in search of Mamma. The others may have. I did not.

After an hour or so, Papà said we should go home. Tomorrow was a school day. And it was late. I remember watching the puffs of smoke burp out from the exhaust pipes of other cars on the road. We slowly inched our way through the neighborhoods of Hyde Park, at that time not exactly the safest place to be at night. I slowly realized that we had passed the same house twice now. I started to pay attention. Same street. Same turns. It was then that Papà stopped the car and pulled over.

Our human GPS had broken down.

"*Ma, bambini, dove siamo?*" Papà, in a very nervous, frightened voice, was asking us where we were.

That shook me to my core. He never got lost. And here, finally, Mamma had succeeded in breaking him. He no longer knew the way.

I started to cry. I just couldn't help it.

Cathy said, "I can't believe it. You're crying. You never cry. I thought you were a robot or something."

My sister always had a knack for saying things to make you feel like crap. And for missing things that were obvious if you were looking and wanted to see them. I did cry. But I made sure no one was around to witness it. Crying was a weakness, a vulnerability that exposed me to predators and opened a door to my getting hurt—more than I already had been. Which is why I so hated myself for breaking down in the car that day, and in this particular instance, not only for reasons specific to me but for what it would do to Papà.

"*Paolamia, non piangere.*" Papà turned to look at me.

I couldn't stand doing this to him. My crying added to his feelings of failure; I could see it in his eyes. He kept telling me over and over not to cry. But he could not console me.

Eventually, we found our way home—exactly how much later, I'm not sure, but enough time had passed to allow Mamma to beat us to it.

Yup.

We turned the key in our front door, pushed it open, and walked inside, and there, sitting on our olive green–and-gold couch, with a single table lamp illuminating her face—a face of forcefully restrained rage—with her right leg crossed over her left, her foot dancing to its own angry beat, sat Mamma.

Every one of us froze.

I'm sure we all shared the same thoughts, the same emotions.

Fear.

Panic.

Dread.

And, at least for me, comical disbelief. How the hell had she escaped? How had she gotten here? How had she given the slip to everybody from hospital authorities to police officers? How?

At most, I would learn that when I left Mamma's hospital room for a moment, she fell to her knees, begging Ross to help her escape. He could not refuse. But the details of how? To this day, I really don't know.

Mamma stayed in that spot, on the couch, all night long. Screaming. Threatening. Cursing. Nothing could drown out the shrill of her voice. She kept saying she would blow up the house with all of us in it. Set fire to us all. I kept hearing the *click-click-click* of the oven burner being turned on. I couldn't wait until the morning. I wanted to get out of the house. And I wanted everybody else out, too. It was the only way I would know we'd all have a chance of surviving at least one more day.

I don't remember the next morning. I'm sure that at some point I fell asleep. I'm sure that I got myself to school. And I'm sure that when I left, everybody was still alive. Beyond that, I remember nothing. Nothing but a string of days and weeks with more of the same.

Mamma must have slept during the day while the rest of the family slogged through work and school. At night, when it was time for us to retire, that's when she would come alive.

I wondered if it was all part of her master plan. I knew she had to have one. That was obvious from her having given the hospital the slip. I wondered if, just like those summertime cicadas, she planned on buzzing, buzzing, buzzing every night, all night long, until she succeeded in exhausting us to the point where we were incoherent and ultimately driven crazier than she.

I thought about that saying "If you can't beat 'em, join 'em." Part of me thought we should. Joining in the madness seemed as if it might be a lot easier.

I made it through the next morning at school but had no idea what, exactly, I had made it through. The only thing I do recall is how muddied my mind seemed to be. I felt as if I were in a fog. I tried to focus on whatever was in front of me. I tried to stop all my thoughts from happening all together. Mamma. School. Gunner. Work. Money. Papà. I needed them to stand in line. Take a number. One at a time, please!

I began to notice something else, too. Everywhere I went, I could hear that song playing. Those drums and the whispers asking what was going on. Fleetwood Mac's *Tusk* was stalking me.

Joel had it playing on his little transistor radio in the bus on the way to school. Sister Mary Jude, the full-habit nun who managed all administrative support at St. Scholastica, was playing it in her office when I arrived late one day and needed a tardy slip. Even worse, I had forgotten to wear a bra that day. Under my white blouse. Sister Mary Jude handed me a loaner pullover—after chastising me, of course, as if I had done it on purpose. How could I explain that I wasn't trying to be sexy or perverted but rather was merely attempting to function without sleep?

I wondered if the song stalking was really just the same thing: my imagination playing tricks on me, due to my missing out on shut-eye. I thought it as much as I knew it wasn't true. Other people heard it, too. I could see their lips moving, their bodies pulsing with the beat, could even hear them humming along. It was as if the universe had decided to play some cruel joke by having one of Gunner's favorite tunes follow me around, purposely mocking me.

Someone had told me that "tusk" was slang for "penis." The thought made me nauseous. And hearing that song following me around was forcing me to keep thinking of him and it.

I wished I had given Gunner that album. That's what I should have done for his fortieth-birthday gift. And even as I wished it, thinking it would have cleared up any misunderstandings about the gift I meant him to have, I now wondered if it would have. Or if it—along with what I said, how I acted, what he saw in me, what he heard, what he smelled—would not have mattered, or changed how he'd changed me forever.

I tried to shut out that song.

Joy the lunch lady had it playing on her little transistor. Every time I came down for lunch, it played. I was beginning to think it was a conspiracy: Somehow, she knew. And she was taunting me.

The fact that I was even thinking that, so similar to Mamma's thoughts, scared me.

It can't be, I told myself. *Can't.*

Joy was like a hip grandma. Logic finally dictated that whatever radio station she had that box set to must have the song on some sort of lunchtime loop. Still, smaller than a shoebox, sitting on the metal folding chair, plugged into the outlet just before the turn into the lunchroom, it taunted me. I dared myself to kick it quiet. I could easily have pretended to trip on the power cord, accidentally smashing it and the sounds it made to pieces. But I couldn't do it. Not to Joy.

I had a growing list of people in charge who shouldn't be. People who deserved to be kicked and smashed to pieces. And when I was alone, when I allowed myself to think the worst of thoughts, I envisioned hurting them, as much as, if not more than, they hurt me. But before I lost control, I reined in my rage and convinced myself that the bad was not in them but in me. Somehow I always felt deep down that they did what they did, acted the way they acted, only because of something I had done. I could always rationalize away their behavior because I believed that no matter what I did, I was responsible. I was to blame.

As I approached the lunch line, the music getting louder, I tried to focus on Joy's frizzy hair or her smile, the one she tried so hard to stretch thin and stern, only to betray her true self with a wink and her usual singsongy salute—"Eat hearty, girls"—as she extended her hand to check our passes and let us by. I wasn't sure what would happen if the authorized lunch time stamped on our respective passes didn't match up with the clock on the wall. And I would never know, because inside that school, I still followed the rules.

I stood at the counter, overlooking the hot-lunch offerings of the day. I had money in my pocket to buy whatever I wanted. And, creature of comfort when it came to food, I wanted the chicken soup. It was called "homemade," but I was pretty sure it was little more than doctored Lipton. Still, it reminded me of Mamma's *pastina* and soup. Any kind of soup always made me feel warm and loved. Especially when I wasn't.

Some of my favorite soups were those we made at the donut shop. They came in giant cans and all sorts of flavors: chicken noodle, beef barley, beef vegetable, chili. On Friday afternoons when I raced from school to work, not having had time to eat dinner, the first thing I did the moment I was left alone at the donut shop was pour myself a bowl of whatever soup was already simmering. I loved the way I could feel it sliding down my throat and into my tummy. And I could eat as much of it as I wanted, as long as no one was around to see. I also started sneaking one giant can out pretty much every other week, especially after I realized that the brand name of that soup was the same as the kind my *papà* made at the factory where he now worked. It was called LeGoût. Papà was able to buy the soups at an employee discount monthly, but he never had to, after a while, because I made sure to restock our basement pantry, free of charge. And neither he nor anybody else ever noticed or asked about it.

Papà didn't much like working at the factory, at least not as much as he'd liked having his own barbershop. But he had no choice. He'd never made it past the third grade. Cutting hair and giving men a close shave didn't bring in the money it once had. We also needed to cover Mamma's mounting medical bills, so taking a factory job was what he had to do. And I was glad knowing that he never had to use his paycheck to buy what I could get on my own.

The other girls at the lunch table are a blur to me now. I never was part of a clique. I had friends, but on other-than-school nights, I was working and they were not. When I'd first started at the donut shop, they had come to visit, mostly for free donuts. But lately I had found myself increasingly alone, and yet so busy trying to juggle all the balls in the air that I rarely allowed myself time to feel lonely. In a great many ways, as much as I may have been aware of what was going on around me—realizing that some of the girls were "together," as in coupled up with boys or even with other girls; knowing that a lot of the girls smoked in the parking lot behind the school the minute the last bell rang; learning that Jackie, one of my best friends, had gotten pregnant and was being kicked out of school—I just didn't get involved. Whether by choice or because of the sheer volume of all else that was already on my plate, I made sure to keep my distance. I viewed it as self-preservation.

I remember phone call after phone call from Jackie. I cringed at every ring. I hated taking the calls. I couldn't stand her crying. She needed a friend to tell all her secrets to; I needed not to know, lest I accidentally share with her all of mine. Part of me also struggled with any sort of real empathy. Jackie drank. She smoked. More than just cigarettes. She had a longtime boyfriend, Keith, whom she willingly had sex with and was now going to have a baby with. Every single thing she did was for herself, to have fun—consequences be damned. Everything I did seemed always to be to help others. The family. I seemed damned with consequences for things I was accused of but had never actually done. And the one time I'd had sex hadn't been what I had dreamed it to be.

"So shut up, Jackie. Just shut up. Because you don't know how lucky your messed up life really is!"

"What did you say . . . ?" Jackie choked out the words between sobs.

Oh my God. What did I say? Did I say that out loud? I stared at the phone receiver.

"How could you say that to me? What kind of friend are you?"

Click.

Conversation ended.

As much as I felt like shit, my entire body melted, relieved to have shut out the noise.

Jackie disappeared for a while after that. She no longer came to the donut shop.

I tried to care. But I didn't.

And my lack of caring continued, as Sister Celeste noted. I had been taking piano lessons at St. Scholastica. It was one thing I truly wanted to do, and gladly stole extra money to pay for. I was even willing to be subjected to the nun I and others called Sister Callous Face, a pent-up tyrant eager to ridicule and administer corporal punishment. One of her favorite rituals was to force me and everyone else to clip our fingernails to the nub. Sometimes she did it herself, making sure she nicked you with the scissors while she did.

I had come to the realization that I could not keep up, not even with the things I loved. Practicing piano was one of those things. I could not devote the time necessary to it, despite the pleasure I got from it. And I couldn't allow myself to be bad at it. I had no choice but to quit.

I arrived late for my lessons, in part because I really didn't want to give it up. Bad move on my part. I imagined myself entering the room, apologizing for being late. Sister Celeste would have some derogatory comment to make, something to the tune of, *Well, not that it would matter anyway . . .* or *Well, I was hoping you arrived at the same conclusion as everyone else: that you should quit.*

That way, I could just respond, "Okay, I quit." That way, it would be more her doing than mine.

But on that day, no sooner had I gotten the words out—"Sister, I'm sorry I'm late. I'm also sorry I won't be able to continue with my piano lessons"—than Sister Callous Face literally grabbed me by my collar and dragged me out the door. She then shoved me across the hall and against the row of metal lockers.

"The world does not revolve around you, Ms. Milana," she spat out. The words echoed in the hallway.

Even then I thought to myself, *Tell me something I don't know.* But I held my tongue and tried to hold back my tears. I yanked away from her and ran down the hall. I knocked on the office door of the dean, Sister Joanna. I was going to file a complaint.

"What do you expect me to do, Paolina?"

"What?" I stood there, my mouth open, even though part of me had expected her to respond this way. "I expect you to talk to her about what she did." I raised my voice, knowing it would do little good. Authority figures I had encountered all seemed to stick together; why would an order of nuns behave any differently?

Sister Joanna slowly shook her head and said, "There's an outstanding bill. Next quarter is already past due."

That response, I had not expected.

I immediately shut down and left her office, knowing I had been beaten. I had lost.

I sloughed my way through the slush on my way to the bus stop, not really wanting to go home but having no choice.

The bus stopped in front of me. Joel opened the doors to let me in. I was his regular.

"Hey there, isn't it a bit late to be out on a school night?"

I had been working on an extracurricular project, I explained.

We chatted casually, until he extended his invitation.

"Hey, you know I'm having a Christmas party of sorts at my place. Maybe you wanna come over?"

My heart sank.

Without even pausing to breathe, I responded, "Sure. Maybe. Who else is invited?"

"Just a bunch of friends, neighbors. My wife throws this party every year."

Phew. I let out a deep breath I hadn't realized I was holding. I found myself no longer sure of friend versus foe, what to expect and what would be unexpected. I also continued doubting myself, wondering what others interpreted my words and actions to really mean.

When I smiled at Gunner, when I watched him lick strawberry icing from his lips, did it mean something? Was I communicating something? Did I mean to? I needed to focus on being the robot. *Be the robot.*

We had arrived at my stop. Joel had given me the 411 on the party. He had handed me a red invitation. That made it more official. Like it really was what he said it was.

I made no promises but said I would try to make it. He bid me good night, telling me to get straight to bed, it was a school night. I exited the bus, crossed the street, and walked the three blocks or so to my house, wondering—as I had wondered so many times before—if someone was just being friendly to me or if there was something wrong with me because I kept attracting people who wanted something from me that I wasn't sure I could give or even wanted to.

Scarlet

"*Paola. Paolamia. Svegliarti.*"

I struggled to make my body acknowledge, let alone move in response to, my *papà*'s plea for me to wake up. His voice was deeper than its usual deep, quieter than even an early-morning whisper should be. I loved how he called me Paolamia—his Paola.

"*Dai, Paoletta. Alzarti.*"

We had now crossed over from "wake up" to "get up." And while his words were still melodic in tone, I could sense the urgency straining every one of them. I had no idea what time it was, but even with my eyes still shut, I could tell from the lack of any hint of morning light trying to seep in through my lids and wake me that even the break of dawn was still snoozing away.

I opened my eyes just enough to see his face hovering above me. His gap-toothed smile was pulled into a tight-lipped frown. His eyes looked glassy.

I sprang to sit up in bed. "*Che cè, Papà?*" I swung my feet over the side and stood. Papà turned without a word, and in silence I followed him out of my bedroom, down the stairs, and into the kitchen, where the lights barely illuminated the darkness. An attaché case, what we all knew as Papà's *valigetta*—the all-important "little suitcase" that held vital documents, including loan papers, Social Security cards, birth certificates, and more—sat squarely in the center of our white

Formica table, framed beautifully by the gold scrolls that decorated it.

Papà motioned to me to take a seat. He poured a cup of coffee. As he added cream and sugar, just the way I liked it, I wanted to tease him: How dare he not have waited for me to make the coffee? Didn't he know I made it best and we'd just have to make it all over again? But I knew better. I watched as he held the cup in one hand, swirled its contents with a teaspoon in his other, and stared down into the liquid, as if mesmerized by the tiny whirlpool he was creating.

"Papà?"

He lifted his head. "*Siamo mezzi guai.*"

Papà's stating the obvious—that we were in the middle of trouble—made me see red. Did he not think I already knew this? Was this some James Bond, Agent 007 moment, complete with attaché, when he was going to unveil the mess we were in? I stared at him almost dumbfounded, knowing that he didn't have a clue just how messed up things really were.

He handed me my cup of coffee, and I drank it down, almost in one giant gulp. It didn't matter how it tasted—I needed to swallow down the words that were fighting to vomit their way out my mouth.

He sat down next to me; opened *la valigetta*; took out some looseleaf ruled paper, a pen, and some other printed documents, almost carbon-copy-looking, with a bunch of holes down one side; and placed it all in front of me. A quick glance, and I realized they were from the hospitals we frequented on behalf of Mamma.

My *papà* rested his hand on top of mine, and we locked eyes. Usually, his brown eyes mirrored mine, but today they looked as if they were about to melt away, dissolve right in front of me. His chiseled features, that ruling Roman nose, also had somehow grown soft, sunken—like quartz or limestone after pressure and time rub them down, shaping them until they lose their edges.

He needed me to write another letter. He said the insurance company was refusing to pay some of Mamma's bills. I would need to study up on some medical and legal terminology. We needed to fight them. I needed to.

My *papà*'s English was passable. He made himself understood. He could carry on a conversation. His accent didn't get in the way of verbal communication. But the written word didn't come as easily to him. He spelled even simple words, such as "bye," as "bay"; "beach" became "bitch." It wasn't his fault. The Italian language didn't even have spelling as a subject. There was no need for it. Every word was spelled as it sounded, according to clearly defined rules that came with only rare exceptions. English, on the other hand, had more exceptions than rules. So, since the age of ten, I had been his ghostwriter. It had been easy for me right from the start. And in the past several years, I had perfected my craft: I wrote and sounded just like—no, better than—an authoritative adult. Somebody who knew her shit. Somebody you didn't want to mess with. Rarely, if ever, did one of my letters fail to get what it asked for—no, demanded. This letter would be no different. The only challenge here was time. Papà had to respond with something postmarked by today. He had to leave the house for work by 5:00 a.m. That gave me about an hour.

I was done in less than twenty minutes.

"*Brava!*" Papà beamed at the letter and then brightened more when he looked at me. "*Vuoi un biscotto?*"

Before I could answer, Papà placed two Stella D'oro Almond Toast biscotti within reach and refreshed my coffee. I had inherited Mamma's love of dunking them into coffee until they were so soft, they looked as if they would break off and drop right into the cup. But we'd both rescue our biscotti just seconds before they fell, and we'd gobble them up, coffee dribbling down our chins.

Papà kept talking. I kept eating. He said Mamma had had a very bad night. She had been telling us for days that things in the house were missing: candlesticks, serving trays, crystal, pictures, money—anything and everything seemed to just vanish. She wanted to call the police, but Papà wouldn't let her. It didn't make sense, he reasoned, that only one thing would go missing at a time. No thief, not even a stupid one, said Papà, would do that.

Papà's disbelief of Mamma sparked her rage as much as her silence. I wasn't sure which of the two frightened me more. With the former, I always knew where she was and what she was doing. Not so much with the latter.

A few nights prior, she had said that Uncle Joe had come to visit us, back from the grave. She recounted for us how, in the middle of the night, he climbed the stairs and opened her bedroom door. Her eyes lit up as she told us how she saw the outline of his curly hair, her hand passing over her own as she spoke. Uncle Joe wanted his silver platter back, she said. So he took it. Part of Mamma expressed elation at the fact that it was her brother who had been the one taking things. It made her giddy to the point of mania—screaming, laughing, talking out loud to nobody there. Sometimes she'd rant about furnishing Uncle Joe's new home, sometimes about how disgraceful it was for him to have taken back gifts that weren't even his, sometimes about how rude he had been not to have let us know, and to have made us think we were being robbed. Sometimes she'd cry about how sorry she was, and that she hadn't meant to kick him out, to kill him. It went on and on and on.

Until last night.

Papà happened to stumble upon all the loot, stashed atop the rafters in the garage. Or, to be more accurate, he didn't so much stumble upon it as it crashed down upon him, right onto the hood of his car, just as he was pulling into the garage.

He confronted Mamma, showing her the items she claimed had disappeared, accusing her of being the one hiding them. She denied it all. But Papà wouldn't let it go. He said he just couldn't. I nodded. I wanted him not to feel bad, to know I understood.

He told me how she had become uncontrollable. The doctor had given her sleeping pills, a drug she refused to take. Papà said he had snuck them into her dinner the previous night. As he told me the story, he became more animated, acting out how she'd nearly fallen headfirst into her plate, and his eyes lit up with laughter, and there, finally, came the return of his gap-toothed grin.

I laughed along with him. He joked about drugging her every night so that we all could get some sleep. But just as he said it, we both knew that Mamma was too smart for that. We could trick her once, but one shot was all we'd get. And we both knew that tonight, when Papà came home from work, he'd pay, some way, somehow, for what he had done.

"*Grazie, bambina mia.* I tank God for you." Papà planted a kiss on my forehead. He gathered up the letter I had written, now neatly tucked into a stamped, addressed envelope, snapped shut *la valigetta*, and turned to head downstairs toward the garage.

As I raced upstairs, back to my bedroom, I was careful not to wake any still-sleeping giants, thankful for the drugs and for my Papà's smarts. Why hadn't we thought of it before?

I had almost forgotten about it: the red envelope Joel the bus driver had given to me. It had slid between my dresser and my bed. Actually, it was more like under my bed, a place I never gave much thought to, not even as a place to hide, either things or myself. I guess had the envelope not been red, maybe I would never have seen it peeking out, just a tiny corner of it winking at me, begging for me to notice it. For sure, then I would never have opened it. And had I never opened it, there's no way I would ever have done what I ended up doing.

I suppose it was a good thing I was the one to retrieve that invitation. God knows what would have happened if Mamma had found it. Good thing she no longer cleaned the house much. She probably would have thought a little bit of what I thought when Joel first gave it to me. She would have thought that it was some sort of proof that I was what she believed me to be: the daughter who was beyond boy-crazy, doing it with anyone and everyone, including my own brother and Papà.

I sat on the edge of my bed, caressing the somewhat scratchy, construction-like paper, and resolved to go and prove her wrong.

Christmas was around the corner. How different it felt from last year. The strawberry-iced donuts were still strawberry-iced, but Mr. Kumar had tried to make them redder in color so they'd be more attractive to holiday-celebrating donut eaters. Instead of looking festive, they just looked sort of angry to me. And they tasted terrible. Whatever he put in the frosting made it horribly bitter. Nobody ever returned one, mind you, at least that I knew of, but I bet Gunner would have. He would have spit it out the minute he took the first bite. I thought about how that would have been pretty much half the donut, if not the whole thing, the way he devoured them. Maybe it would have been so stuffed into his mouth that he would have had to just swallow it down, bitter taste and all. That would have made him see red—his face, I bet, would have turned all red, so much so that his strawberry-blond hair would have looked white. Old.

The envelope was sealed. I wondered if Joel had licked it himself, or if it was his wife's spit that had made it stick. Whoever's spit it was, it didn't leave even a tiny edge free for me to fit my pinky through. Maybe if I had one of those fancy letter openers, I could slip it in and slice it open without doing much damage. But I didn't. All I had nearby was a pencil in my book bag. I rummaged around for it, found it, poked the point into the very corner edge of the envelope, and figured if I swept it upward in one quick motion, I could open it up without totally ruining the entire thing.

I was wrong.

Not only did I mangle the envelope, but I managed to tear apart a bit of the actual invitation itself.

Well, at least now it was open.

I pulled the invitation out, pushed aside the blankets and rumpled sheets from my bed, placed it down on top of my mattress, and smoothed it out as much as I could. I tried to fit back together the little piece that had torn off, but I didn't have any glue or tape handy, so it just sort of floated in and out of place with every move I made on my bed.

The words were all written by hand, not preprinted. I had sort of expected a real invitation to look more real. This one had a swirly kind of script, like calligraphy, but worse. And as with like the spit, I wondered whose handwriting this was.

"Holiday party." That's what it said. Not "Christmas party."

I wondered if Joel was Jewish. He had to know I was Catholic. The uniform screamed it.

This coming Friday night. That's when it was. I hadn't yet missed it.

Some place called Cary, Illinois. I had never heard of it.

Other writing—smaller, block-print kind of writing, upside down—was on the other side. I flipped the card to read it. The little piece floated to the floor, but I left it there.

Directions. The smaller, upside-down print told me what I needed to do. But these weren't driving directions; they were train and bus routes to get from school, or, to be more exact, to get from where Joel's bus picked me up after school to Joel's house—a three-hour, one-way trip, according to what Joel had written.

That couldn't be, I thought. *No way.*

I looked it up in the library at school. Cary was over fifty miles away from St. Scholastica. It was a little closer to where I lived, but just barely. So, wow, three hours one way was right.

I knew it was ridiculously far. I wondered why Joel would have taken so much time mapping out my route—not a driving route, but one on public transportation—and assumed that I wouldn't get someone to drive me. He'd even gone so far as to expect me to come alone. I could see the red flag waving at me, begging me to pay attention. But I chose to ignore it. In some screwed-up way, I reasoned that if I did heed those warnings, that somehow meant that I believed Mamma—all she thought, all she said—was right.

I carefully mapped out my route. I would leave school on Friday, run to catch the earlier bus, and be at Joel's house by 7:00 or 7:30 p.m., just in time for the party's official start. I would pack party clothes and change at some gas station or some McDonald's that I'd surely find along the way, in between bus and train transfers. Oh, but first I had to remember to call the donut shop from school no later than noon on Friday; I'd say I was sick and was being sent home, so that it would seem more real. That would give Mr. Kumar three hours to either get a replacement or get in from wherever he was himself. And it would give me maybe an hour or so at the party before I had to turn around and head home. And I would tell my *papà* that I would get a ride home from work with . . .

I thought about it for a bit. With whom? Ross and Cathy drove. They actually split the use of a car between them. But I sure as hell couldn't ask either of them to come get me and keep it a secret.

There was no one I could ask for help.

In the past, I could have asked Gunner.

I'd have to make something up. A name. A person. I would just make it up. Maybe I'd say I had been asked to train a new kid and she'd volunteered to drive me home. And then I would say that she was terrible at the job and that Mr. Kumar had fired her before Papà even thought of wanting to meet her.

Or . . . I could keep her alive. And maybe whenever I needed her to take me home so that I could do something I really wanted to do, she'd be my ride.

That sounded brilliant to me. And so was born Marcie. She was Jewish, I decided. Seventeen years old. Legal driving age. I used Dahlia as my model for her. Marcie worked weekday shifts. Those were her normal work hours. That's what I'd say. That's why Papà would never get to meet her.

Brilliant.

A few moments after I gave birth to Marcie, however, it dawned on me that a seventeen-year-old would need to be in school on weekdays.

Maybe not so brilliant.

But a few moments later, I had the solution. I decided Marcie was a dropout. She had to work because she'd gotten pregnant. Like my friend Jackie. Only Jackie had to go to a public school. Marcie, I decided, had come from a public school but had been sort of flunking out anyway, so she'd just bailed.

Things were starting to get complicated. I worried I couldn't keep the lies straight. But I decided this was just another red flag to ignore, and came to the conclusion that I was back to being brilliant.

Everything was going according to plan that Friday. I couldn't believe how easy it all was. Why hadn't I done this before? I didn't know where I would have gone or what I would have done, but now that I knew it was possible, that I could get away with it, I was determined to do it more.

There was only one tiny snag in my master plan.

I was lost.

I somehow had gotten onto the wrong route. None of the stops we passed was familiar to me; not one name matched any of the names on my map. And even if one did I wouldn't know it, because I couldn't make out most of the signs we passed; we were traveling so fast.

I started breathing like I couldn't catch my breath. It was dark outside. It was already past seven. I was shaking a little bit. Panic had set in. I could feel the tears starting to come.

I raised my hand and grabbed for the drooping chord to ring the bell and stop the bus. I had to get off, and at the next stoplight I could see through the front window that the area was busy enough and well-lit enough and there was a McDonald's in sight. Thank God for McDonald's. There had to be a phone somewhere nearby.

Whom would I call? I so wanted to call my *papà*. But I wasn't yet ready to give in to getting the ass kicking of my life, which was exactly what would happen if I did call him.

I pulled the red invitation out of my pocket. My hands were sweaty, and the paper started getting splotchy. I tried to wipe my palms on my jacket. I tried to slow my breathing. *Calm down,* I told myself. *Just find a phone and call the number on the invitation, and maybe Joel will come get you or at least tell you where you are and how to get to him.* Maybe he could have somebody at the party drive over to get me. I couldn't be that far off from where I was supposed to be. I had been so careful.

My tears again threatened to spill.

I ran to the McDonald's. I let out a long breath: a pay phone was right outside. I straightened my invitation so that I could read the numbers and dial. I dropped my bag between my legs and fished out change.

It was ringing. Finally, somebody picked up.

"Hello?" a lady's voice answered.

"Hi. This is Paolina, Joel's friend. I was following his directions to the party tonight, but I think I'm lost."

Silence.

Why wasn't she saying anything? I stammered on.

"I was hoping Joel could . . ."

The lady said only two words but drew each one out, harsh, emphasized: "What party?"

I paused before I answered. My back instinctively stiffened. My throat tightened. I eked out my words slowly and quietly.

"Joel's Christmas—I mean holiday—party. At his house."

Pause. Breathe.

"At least I think this is his house—"

Click.

The phone went dead.

I held the receiver in my hand, still up to my ear, even after the tone changed to an angry *beep-beep-beep.*

I didn't know what to think. Or I knew what to think but I didn't want to think it. At least not what I was thinking, which was exactly what I had thought when Joel had first invited me to his party.

But I still didn't want to believe it.

I hung up. I walked into the McDonald's. I was still in my school uniform. I thought about changing into my party clothes. I had brought with me that red blouse Mamma's client had given her, the one with the shine to it and the bow at the top. I had so wanted to wear it. Just once. I thought about slipping it on. How smooth and silky soft it would be. The thought of it comforted me, but I decided against it. It would only lead to more trouble, especially if Mamma saw me in it. Not worth the risk. I thought about changing into my donut shop uniform. I would have to before I made it back home anyway. But then I figured I didn't want to do that, either. Of all the outfits I had with me, none was stranger danger–proof. And I suddenly felt like an easy target, easy prey.

How was I going to get back home? Where was I? I looked around. I had no clue.

The girl behind the McDonald's counter was asking to take my order. I had absentmindedly wandered over to where she was. I figured I might as well order something. I was actually pretty hungry. And I needed to get it together. Swallow down the tears and the fear.

I looked at my watch. I had been on the road four-plus hours. I had maybe fifteen minutes to shovel down some food, maybe a Coke, to stay awake and alert, and get back home in less time than it had taken to get to where I had no clue I was.

Call Papà, the voices inside my head started shouting. *Call Papà.*

I wanted to. God, I wanted to.

The girl behind the counter asked to take my order again. I rattled off my favorites: Big Mac, large fries, Coke, apple pie, please. And, as calmly as I could, I asked her for the address of the McDonald's.

She didn't know.

I wanted to explode.

"You don't know?" I was about to say more, but then I tried to think of the address of the donut shop and realized I had no clue what that was, either.

I took a breath, finally stammering out, "What town am I in?"

"Crystal Lake," she said, smiling, handing me my food and drink on a plastic tray.

I sat at the nearest table. I felt safer closer to the girl and the front counter. I ate, and while I did, I scoured my map. My shoulders came down from my ears a little bit when I spotted CRYSTAL LAKE in big, bold print and then saw CARY, in much smaller print, two stops earlier. I had overshot my destination.

Okay. Okay. Not so bad, I thought, trying to console myself.

It didn't matter anyway. It was way too late to do anything but try to get home.

While I stuffed fries in between the two all-beef patties and sesame-seed buns, then stuffed them together into my mouth, I thought about Joel, the lady on the phone, and the party that wasn't. I ran scenarios through my mind.

Maybe she went to get Joel and somebody else hung up the line.

Maybe the party was canceled. Joel didn't get an official RSVP from me, so he didn't think to tell me.

Wow. What would have happened had I shown up? What would she have done then?

And what was supposed to have happened if she wasn't there?

I tried to shut off my mind. But I couldn't.

My logical self kept mocking me, pushing me: *She didn't accidentally hang up; the party wasn't canceled, because there was no party. Don't you get it? Joel is a creep.* That's what I kept telling myself. Along with, *You're such an idiot.*

Still I argued with myself. I told myself Joel was my friend. The lady was just embarrassed. She didn't know they had missed telling a guest the party had been canceled. I told myself she hadn't meant to hang up on me but had accidentally dropped the line. I told myself it was all a misunderstanding, and I was sure Joel would explain it to me the next time he drove me home on the bus.

I told myself I was right.

Even when I knew I was wrong.

Solitaire

I don't really know how I made it home that night. I don't remember the ride back. I don't recall changing into my donut-shop uniform. I don't know how I found my way. But somehow I did. I made it home. True, I was a little later than I probably was expected, but as I got closer and closer to my house, I concocted stories to cover me. I decided that Marcie would be to blame. She needed to learn how to clean everything up, and she was so slow, it just took longer. I carried it out a bit in my head, realizing that this would serve me well if later I had to fire her. I would add that Marcie didn't know how to get me home and wasn't the greatest driver, and that was another part of why I was later than usual.

But when I reached the door to my house, noticing that the drapes were drawn, bracing myself for whatever was on the other side, expecting to get my ass kicked the moment I entered, I realized the focus was not on me.

Some other something was more important.

Ross had gotten fired from his job at the grocery store, for stealing.

Flashes of him teaching me when I was no older than five or six how to steal Matchbox cars clouded my vision. Surely, I thought, this was equally innocent. Not Ross.

Later, my brother would tell me what happened. He would say that he and his best friend, Julian, were left alone at the store, as usual, to unload a truck of meat. Because it was so close to Christmas, they joked with each other about how much they'd love to eat this one turkey as they tossed it into the bin for stocking. And their mouths watered as they talked about the prime ribs and the beef tenderloins, and how both their families needed a real Christmas this year, and how much it would mean to bring home Christmas dinner . . .

Before they even realized it, they were throwing meat into their own cars. And being watched as they did.

I was scared that Ross would have to go to jail, but Ross's boss loved him. He told Ross and Papà, whom he had called down to come get Ross, that he would not press charges but had to fire Ross.

I knew my brother felt horrible about what he had done. Every now and then, he'd just look at me and tell me again how his boss reacted: "I was the last person he ever thought would steal from him. That's what he kept saying."

I didn't know what to say to my brother. I knew he had stolen. Not just toy cars. He was a thief. He had lost his job because of it and was lucky he wasn't going to jail. He understood that he had let someone down who cared for him, trusted him, maybe even loved him.

I understood why he had done it. I understood that they, too, had let him down.

At least, that's how I felt.

At the donut shop, I had become forgettable. Gunner didn't visit. Friends rarely did. The place that used to be filled with life and sort of like a stage for me to be alive was now empty, more often than not. Even regulars had stopped being so regular. And I had started being irregular, forgetful, too.

Like, I never used to fall flat on my back when the cleanup guys mopped the floors. I used to sort of skate or glide, almost acrobatically, from the donut displays to the end of the counter, expertly juggling coffee and donuts and soup, regardless of how wet the floor might be. But no longer. Now I couldn't seem to keep my footing.

I also couldn't keep track of where everybody was at every moment—a key component to being a good thief. A couple of times, after having just pocketed a payment for donuts and coffee at the counter, I'd turn around to see Mr. Kumar just turning the corner, coming out of the back room. I wasn't sure what, if anything, he saw. But I was sure that I was losing my edge.

My game was off. It had been for a while. Six months or so. Ever since Gunner did what he did.

Maybe I was just too old for it. All of it. My fifteenth birthday had come and gone. That Woodstock Willie groundhog had come out to see his shadow, though I can't remember whether he predicted six more weeks of winter or not. I just remember that winter lingered on.

When spring finally started to show itself, I thanked God as I stared out the windows, wishing I was . . . who, what, where, I didn't know.

I wiped down the counters. I pulled out and dumped the old coffee grounds from the machine, replacing them with fresh grounds and starting up another pot. For whom, I couldn't say. But I wanted to be ready. I still secretly wished.

I turned up my radio. At least I could count on that as a constant companion. I sang out loud. I missed singing, being in front of an audience. At St. Scholastica, other girls really knew how to sing and even dance. In my head, I knew I could belt out a tune at least as well as they could. I did in church at St. Peter's. And I was the star ballerina when I was little, so I knew I could dance probably as well.

But no way could I do rehearsals and performances, amid all else I had to do. Even if I wanted to.

I pretended to be Streisand, talking about her lover not bringing her flowers. I gave Gunner the role of Neil Diamond.

I tried to silence the voices in my head telling me how pathetic I was, and just to focus on the music. But the more time ticked by, the more I got lost inside my mind.

Why?

That's what I wanted to ask Gunner.

I just wanted to know.

What did he think? What was he thinking?

What had I done to make him think it? To make him do what he did to me?

I wanted to say I was sorry. I should have been ready. I should have known.

The rattrap in the corner of the back room grinded its gears, making me jump. I focused in on it. Then focused in on me. I had made my way back there, without even meaning to. My fingers were dripping with strawberry frosting. Some of it was splattered across the top of my uniform. I licked my lips and tasted it. The vats of frosting were all in front of me, lids off. I realized I had been eating the frosting with my fingers, right from the giant containers. And even now, conscious of it, I couldn't stop. I moved over to the maple, then the vanilla. Like some vampire lapping up pools of blood to sustain life, I drank.

Powerless.

It had become a mindless behavior. Eating. Not just at the donut shop. A lot of the money I made—stole—now went to bingeing. Long John Silver's was a favorite eatery. I didn't even have to ask them any longer to give me an extra serving of those deliciously greasy little bits of batter that fall off the pieces of fried fish, officially called "crumbs"; I had become a regular, and they had a basket of them already waiting for me every time I visited.

I ate at the donut shop. I ate at school. I ate at home. In the same day—two, three, four times for every meal. Yet I always felt as if I were on empty. Like one of those donut holes, one of the plain glazed ones that never gets filled.

I knew I was growing in size. I'd had to trade in my work uniform for a bigger one.

Karen never said much about it, except she would pat my behind, telling me I had more of an ass as a white girl than she did as a black girl. Aurora disapproved. She made it quite clear with her raised-eyebrow looks and her point-blank comments about my getting too fat for business. I wasn't quite sure what business Aurora thought we were in.

I made sure never to eat in front of them, always sneaking what I wanted, sometimes even eating standing up in the filthy bathroom.

My school uniform's pleats no longer lay flat but rather resembled the bellows of an accordion stuck on the outward motion.

"*Sei bella, Paolamia. E sè perdesi anche dieci libbre, non potessimo tenere i ragazzi lontano.*"

It killed me to hear Papà say I was beautiful . . . but "if you just lost ten pounds, we wouldn't be able to keep the boys away." He didn't get that every time he said it, I knew I had to gain even more in order to keep the boys away. As big as I was getting, the extra weight seemed to be settling in my boobs and my hips—not where I needed the fat to go—and, as everyone kept telling me, I still had a pretty face. I wasn't yet big enough to stop the attention, which, more often than not, was unwanted. And yet I was too big already for my *papà* to stop talking after he said the words "you're beautiful." Something inside me always cringed when he continued with his "but" statements; I wished he'd just end by saying, "You're beautiful as is."

I dragged myself into the house on a Sunday afternoon. My body felt like a boulder I had to push uphill. I really just wanted to crawl under the covers and sleep.

My older sister, Cathy, stopped at the hallway mirror for one last pretty-girl check. She was about to leave for the movies: *The Deer Hunter*, with Robert De Niro and Meryl Streep, had been out for weeks already. I loved them both and so wanted to see the movie. Ross was going with her, this time legally, since he had recently turned seventeen. Cathy didn't really allow me to tag along. To anything. Not if she could help it. So it was useless for me even to try.

"You're still such a baby," she'd say in her eighteen-year-old-know-it-all voice. Somewhere deep inside me, it made me smile just a little bit to know that, as much of a baby as I might be, I wasn't the one who was still a virgin.

Papà told Cathy she couldn't go unless she took me with her, too. He was even excusing us all from Sunday dinner. And he was offering to give us extra money to "have good time."

It scared me.

I hadn't asked him to make her take me. I hadn't asked for his money, either. Excusing us from Sunday dinner? That meant he would be left alone with Mamma. As much as I wanted to go, I wondered if he wanted us out of the house in order to do away with her. And then I wondered if that would be such a bad thing.

"What about Viny?" I asked.

Papà said she was staying with him and Mamma.

I relaxed a little, and then wondered if my *papà*'s generosity was due to his actually noticing that his consigliere needed a time-out. As much as that comforted me, it also made me feel guilty. Papà had enough on his mind to deal with without adding me to his worries. I needed to get back to pretending everything was okay. I couldn't show what I was feeling. I made a promise to myself that I would try harder and immediately slapped on my happy face, exuding excitement over the prospect of going to the movies and being treated by Papà.

But Cathy was never one to just do as she was told. She put up a great fight, screaming and yelling about how unfair it was being the oldest.

I guess she was sort of right about that. She was the first to have to ask for things we needed and probably shouldn't even have had to ask for. Like an electric typewriter. She got it for us, after months of campaigning, but Mamma slapped her for pushing them to buy it.

I felt sorry for her sometimes. But the more she did things like what she was doing now—campaigning for me *not* to go to the movies with her—the more that feeling went away.

Cathy continued her bitching. She even tried to explain how the movie wasn't really for little kids but then thought better of it, the more Papà started asking questions about just what kind of movie it really was. She finally shut him up by saying that it was a movie with Robert De Niro from *The Godfather*. There were advantages to having ESL parents who weren't really up on American pop culture and what was or wasn't appropriate. And anything with De Niro or anyone from the bible of all movies, as far as Papà was concerned, was good to go.

With the clock ticking, and not wanting to miss the beginning of the movie, Cathy eventually gave in. But she screamed all the way down the stairs, through the hall, and into the garage that she wasn't going to wait, so I had better change my clothes and be in the car before she backed it out of the driveway.

The last movie I had seen had been with Ross. He had taken me to Lincoln Village Theaters to see *The Warriors*. He had bought the tickets while I waited off to the side. Lincoln Village was the right kind of movie house. In a rough part of Chicago's North Side, surrounded by at least a couple of different gangs, it wasn't the kind of place that asked for ID. And that worked well for me.

I still remember those big red lips nearly kissing the microphone, telling the warriors that they had better run for their lives, and that creepy guy clinking the beer bottles, almost singing out that eerie invitation: "Warriors, come out to *plaaaayyyyyy*."

The warriors hadn't done anything wrong. They'd been falsely accused—innocents who spent the entire two hours defending themselves.

I knew exactly how they felt.

We drove into the parking lot of the Old Orchard Theaters in Skokie. This was Cathy's right kind of movie house: upscale, clean, suburban, legal. The kind that checked ID.

It wasn't mine.

I hid around the corner, sitting on the curb, waiting for Cathy and Ross to bring me my ticket so we could go inside together.

I waited. And waited.

I wasted that entire weekend waiting.

Finally, Ross was walking toward me. The sun had already started setting and was shining right in my eyes, so I couldn't see his face too well. All I could see was that he was alone. I stood up.

"They won't let you in," he said. "Not without an adult."

I argued that Cathy was eighteen, which made her an adult; didn't that matter?

My brother said the man in charge had said it had to be a parent or guardian.

I silently took stock of all the parents and guardians I had encountered. Inside, I laughed at those labels. I wondered if a forged note might do the trick. Or maybe I could ride up in a squad car, sirens blaring in police-escort fashion. Would they let me in then?

"Come on. We'll come back to get Cathy later." My brother moved behind me and started teasingly shoving me toward the car.

I wasn't in the mood to be teased. I suppose I should have been thankful that Ross didn't just leave me to sit outside in the car until the movie was over, that he chose to forfeit seeing it because of me. But I wasn't.

Something inside me clicked that day. Something shut off for good. I realized that there was no rhyme, no reason, to any of it. Why I kept trying to make sense of it all was beyond me. Even asking why was a waste of breath. I'd never get the answers I wanted. Because it didn't matter. Nothing mattered. There were no rules. There was no right or wrong. Whether you did or didn't, nobody was paying attention. Nobody cared.

I still did, though. Care. As hard as I tried not to, I couldn't help it.

At school, I cared still. I tried always to have the right answers for most of the teachers. Always the best. Always the brightest. Always to get noticed. For something good. Something that mattered. So that I would matter.

I clung to the consistent, predictable normalcy of the classroom. I read the books. Did the homework. Got asked the questions. Spit back the answers. It came so easily to me.

Ms. Uzarski was my Advanced Algebra teacher. Classmates would kid that she and I were like this—they'd wrap their two fingers around each other, crossing them—and we were. Ms. U's fingers chalked out formulas on the blackboard almost as quickly as she erased them. I saw this as a game. One I was determined to win. One upon which I focused with laser precision, not daring to miss a moment, lest I miss a step in her lightning-fast calculations and lose my way. While I could see on the other girls' faces the registering of complete confusion, their twisted brows and puzzled expressions served only to strengthen me, making me feel more powerful, smarter, than anyone else in the room.

I was in control. I was a winner. And no one thought otherwise.

Except for me. Deep down.

When I was out of the classroom or out of any place where I was not performing to applause, I ate. And the busier I kept myself, the less time or energy I had to think about it.

In many ways, the days when I went to school and then had to hustle to work—either to the donut shop or to babysit—were more restful to me. I didn't have to deal with Mamma for a few hours more; I didn't have to make small talk with classmates with whom I seemed to have very little in common; I didn't have to engage with anyone who needed to know more about me than I wanted her to know. The more I raced, the less chance there was for secrets to be spilled, the less chance anybody could catch me to hurt me.

I raced into the donut shop that Friday afternoon, but from the moment I entered through the doors, the angel bells accompanying my arrival, something inside me knew I had been caught. And it had nothing to do with the fact that Mr. Kumar was screaming at me.

"Go! Get out of here!"

They were waiting for me in the back room. The rest of them: Karen, Officer James Brown, and Gunner.

I was being dismissed—fired—from the donut shop. In truth, I was being arrested. I think it was the first time I'd heard the words "grand theft." I had gotten cocky. I had gotten careless. I cared less. I had paid attention to numbers, numbers on the little round dial that *click-click-clicked* as Mr. Kumar locked away his cash in his office safe. What I had not paid attention to was what I had never seen before: a video camera.

Mr. Kumar's mouth seemed to be foaming as he spit out words about my hands being cut off. Karen's eyes begged me not to betray her. I didn't. I knew I was in big trouble. I had moved from the cash register to the safe, stealing thousands of dollars over a period of time. At least some of it had been caught on video. I saw it, the video cartridge, in Officer Brown's hands. I felt as if everyone and everything were in slow motion. Trapped in that strawberry jelly Gunner loved so much. Officer Brown kept his eyes on the floor, avoiding my gaze. Maybe he knew we were standing in the very place his partner had committed a felony. Maybe he was getting off on imagining whatever tale he'd been told. Or maybe, for just a second, he thought about how unfair it all was. I know I did.

Gunner took my hands in his, just like when he'd wrapped them in Scotch tape sticky side up, looked right into my eyes, and cinched metal handcuffs around my wrists. He stared at me as if he didn't know who I was. I thought for a moment back to the last time we'd both stood in this same spot. The time I'd looked at him and not known who he was. And in my mind I shouted at him, *Good—that makes us even.*

I rode in the back of his squad car.

Silence.

My mind was blank. Numb.

Gunner's window was open; I welcomed the air rushing in to cool my feverish face.

We stopped at the police station. Officer Brown got out of the car. He nodded to Gunner. He never once looked at me. He shut his passenger door. Gunner drove on.

The police radio chimed in every now and then. Gunner switched it off.

Silence.

So many words ran through my mind. *Rapist. My first. My friend. Betrayal.*

I never noticed or gave any thought to where we were headed. Never bothered to wonder why we were at the police station but only Office Brown got out of the car. Never even noticed we were entering my own neighborhood, until we were in it and stopped right in front of my house. The living room curtains were closed. They were always closed.

Gunner kept the engine running as he opened his door and eased himself out of the squad car. He kept his door open. Then he opened my door, just behind his. He squatted down in front of me. He gently pulled on the handcuffs, bringing my hands right up to his heart. He held them there, palms open, on his chest. He still looked at me, however, with a certain distance. Even though he was looking right through to the core of me, he seemed removed. He took his eyes off me for a moment, enough to put the key into the cuffs' lock and set me free.

As he stood up, he pulled me up and out of the car with him. I followed, no will of my own to do anything but. He moved me far enough away from the door that he could shut it.

I stood there.

He stood there.

Silence.

Finally, he said, "You don't have to worry. I'll take care of this."

Silence.

"Just don't show up around there anymore. Understand?"

I struggled to comprehend what he was saying. *Did he just say he would make it go away?* I stood there, zombie-like, unable or unwilling to respond.

A few moments later, Gunner folded himself back into the driver's seat and shut the door.

My body sort of lunged itself forward a bit, my hand resting on the open window ledge. I had gained maybe fifteen pounds by then, had grown to maybe a size 16 or 18. And I no longer looked like me. In many ways.

"Thank you." I heard the words just barely whisper their way into the warm air. I wasn't sure they came from me.

Gunner took a deep breath. He shifted gears. He turned to look at me, and with a slight shrug of his shoulders whispered back the last words I would ever hear him say to me.

"Six of one, half dozen of another. Now we're even."

Suffocation

I did as I was told. I never went back to the donut shop. I stayed hidden. And silent.

"What are you doing?"

"Nothing."

"What's wrong?"

"Nothing."

"What did he want?"

"Nothing."

It had become my answer for everything.

Nothing.

I pretended, however, to always be doing something. Even when I wasn't. I needed to stay in motion. Stopping for any extended period of time resulted in thinking, and that was the last thing I wanted to do.

"Six of one, half dozen of another. Now we're even."

I needed to focus.

I needed to clear my head.

I needed to get another job.

Before anybody noticed that I no longer had one.

I could not tell my family that I, just like Ross, had been fired for stealing. It would have killed my *papà*. And I couldn't let that happen. Just like I couldn't let missing a tuition payment happen. If I did, there'd be a whole lot of questions asked, questions to which an answer of "nothing" wouldn't be allowed.

The answer was to one day nonchalantly announce to whoever wanted to hear it, "Oh, I left the donut shop; I've moved up to a better job at [blank]." I just needed to fill in that blank. Fast.

I was now fifteen and a half. Closer to sixteen, really. Old enough to legally—with a work permit—get a real job at my real age. Lucky for me, Marshall Field & Company in Skokie's Old Orchard Mall was hiring stock people. And, even luckier, I didn't have to list former experience at the donut shop because, well, no one expected someone not yet even sixteen to have "prior experience" (other than babysitting and typical teen stuff like that). My criminal background would go unchecked.

I interviewed with an old, Oompa Loompa–shaped, Harry Caray glasses–wearing, bushy-browed fellow. The moment my eyes took him in, I thought to myself that he would make a great Disney character: he'd be the cigar-smoking walrus whose bark was worse than his bite. I nicknamed my new supervisor Wally. But to his face, I respectfully addressed him as "sir."

"This is Luke," Wally growled as he led me into the back stockroom, barely pausing long enough to acknowledge my trainer and continuing without ever turning back. "He'll show you what to do," he boomed out over his shoulder, a wisp of cigar smoke following him out.

I stood there in a windowless, concrete-blocked underbelly, surrounded by hundreds of hanging rods draped with plastic-covered garments. Boxes of all shapes and sizes sat on row after row of metal shelves that rose up from the floor and extended nearly to the ceiling. Boxes that didn't fit or were maybe in line to be emptied or filled littered the cement floor, creating a maze for we mice to navigate. Gray iron ladders on wheels were strewn about. It smelled almost like the science lab at school, as if someone were dissecting rats that had been preserved in formaldehyde. Nearby, rolling, freestanding clothing rods shaped like the letter "Z" swayed as if wanting to escape, some completely naked and others half hung with the season's latest fashions, freed from their plastic protectors, steam-pressed, and ready to make their debut on the clothing-department floor.

"Those are called 'Z-rods,'" said the boy named Luke.

He looked my same age, maybe a year or two older, max. Shaggy brown hair. Round brown eyes. Brown pants. Brown shirt. Brown tie. Brown shoes. In a word, Luke was Brown. He was cute in a basset hound kind of way. And as he led me in between rows of what would be my work, explaining skid numbers and department codes and procedures, his mild-mannered, soft-spoken self made me wonder if he had indeed been a lap dog in a previous life.

Luke wasn't anything like Gunner, whom, try as I might, I just couldn't shake from my thoughts.

Gunner was more like Sam Stone. Not in appearance. Not in age. But in something else.

Sam was a neighbor boy, same age as Luke. He seemed to have some sort of radar on me and always showed up whenever I left the house to go babysitting, which I did more often of late, ever since I'd been fired from the donut shop.

Sam sported spiky black hair and brilliant blue eyes; shirts of every color in the rainbow; and shoes that were more like boots, black in color, extending up past his ankles, which were hairy and olive-colored and looked much darker against the white-colored pack of cigarettes he hid there. Sam reminded me of a neon-shocked dragonfly, always darting about.

He made me nervous.

Between my increased babysitting gigs and my new gig at Marshall Field's, I managed to match the money I had pulled in from the donut shop, even though I had to work many more hours to do it.

No one was the wiser.

Except for me.

Working stock at Marshall Field's was quiet. And the quieter it got outside my head, the louder it got inside. My life outside had become nearly silent. There were so many secrets to be kept, and nobody left to tell them to, even if I wanted to. So most conversations I had were with myself, in my head. Sometimes as I walked from home to the bus, or from the bus to school or work, I chatted away to nobody. I'd know I was doing it only when I'd catch somebody looking at me like I was crazy or something. Then I'd immediately shut my mouth, look down at my feet, and get going to wherever I was trying to get.

At the donut shop, I got to talk to people all the time. Even if it was just to take their food orders. But there were others who came in. Other than Gunner. But no one like Gunner. I so missed my conversations with him. But I couldn't think about those any longer. I tried to push him out of my mind the second he popped in. When I couldn't, my chest would squeeze my insides to the point where it hurt even to breathe.

I missed my music, too. It seemed as if God didn't want to talk to me any longer, either. Marshall Field's had that Muzak playing—Barry Manilow, only slower and instrumental—or some classical something that sounded pretty but didn't help me figure out what to do or how to feel. The words were missing. Still, I recognized some of the songs as old favorites from my donut-shop days—I couldn't help it, given that they were on an endless loop—and every time one came on, I made it a point to sing as loudly as I could, though barely a sound came out.

I wondered what Karen and Aurora were doing without me, too. Had they gotten a new girl? Did they treat her like she was their own, too? Or had they already forgotten about me? Had Gunner told them I wasn't in jail? Had he told them why? Had they even cared to ask? Did they think about me as much as I still thought about them? Something inside me doubted it, even though they should have thought of me; after all, we'd always chatted about something, from stupid things Mr. Kumar did to customers who came in and made us laugh or made us mad to cash receipts that needed to make sense.

Working the stockroom at Marshall Field's was pretty safe for me—or I suppose I should say it was safe *from* me. I never had a chance of coming into contact with any cash registers or any money that might find its way into my pocket. Don't get me wrong—I did have to pass cash registers quite often when changing out clothing lines and stocking racks on the floor. Sometimes they'd be open. Every time I thought about it. Stealing. Would anyone notice? Could I get away with it? How would I do it? I even thought about stealing some of the clothes. After all, I was the one who clipped the little sensors to pant-leg seams and shirtsleeves. It swirled around in my brain that until I did that, nobody would even know that that particular article of clothing had ever existed. Oh, sure, the packing slip might suggest otherwise, but there were plenty of times when we counted pieces only to realize we were short.

And I had nothing to do with the shortage.

Oddly, I felt guilty anyway. As if somehow they suspected me of being the reason something was missing. Part of me reasoned that if they already thought that, why not just do it? Then the other part of me made sure to remind me that my ever-growing figure wouldn't be able to fit into any of the clothes I was in charge of stocking, so how stupid would I be to steal what I couldn't even wear?

Mamma would have looked beautiful, I thought, in so many of the clothes that came in. She had lost a lot of weight after she had put a lot on, growing to more than two hundred pounds. She wasn't as tall as I was, by a couple of inches at least, and she had just looked very round and uncomfortable.

The doctors said it was due partially to the meds she was taking and to her always being in bed. Sedentary.

Those same doctors said she was rapidly losing weight because of the meds she was taking and because she was always up at night. Overactive.

I didn't yet know exactly all the names of the medications Mamma was taking or pretending to take. I just knew the side effects: sometimes zombie-ish and catatonic results; sometimes hyper and manic episodes; sometimes nothing at all; sometimes no words to describe the experience.

What I also knew was that I'd come home from work sometimes

and see Papà kneeling beside her as she sat motionless in the bathtub. Whatever it was she was taking was causing her to melt. Literally. She'd have some sort of yellowish-orange goo on her skin. That's how bad her personal hygiene had gotten.

Those same doctors said it was her body excreting fats.

Fats smell. Bad.

Papà would be talking to her softly—about what, I couldn't hear, nor did I really want to. He'd scrub her back, trying to get that substance off her.

I wondered how he could do it. I wondered why he didn't just lock her away, rid himself of her, the way Gunner got rid of me. I wondered if I was more like my *papà*—if I would have it in me to stand by Mamma "till death do us part"—or if I was more like Gunner and would just abandon someone when I'd had enough.

I didn't want to think about it. Because when I did, when it came to Mamma, I knew the answer. I was tired. I wanted out. And I had it stuck in my head that if it weren't for her, I wouldn't be where I was. All that had happened to me wouldn't have happened. I would have grown up and been normal.

Boys sniffing around was normal. Girls wanting boys to sniff around was normal.

Luke, my same-aged trainer and self-appointed number-one fan, thought I was better than just normal. From almost day one, I felt it. His eyes followed me around, especially when I bent over to empty boxes and he could catch a glimpse of my bra or my panties. I didn't show off my underwear on purpose. It was just that I had not gotten clothes that fit me yet; I didn't want to admit I was wearing yet another bigger size. I prayed that not being around all those donuts and frostings and Gunner might help me lose some weight. But months had gone by, and no matter how hard I tried, I just kept eating.

I really didn't mind that Luke followed me around. He was safe. He was sympathetic. He was somebody to talk to. Somebody I could be in control with.

Sometimes, when I didn't feel like hanging clothes, I'd get Luke to do my work. I figured out that if I wore something that maybe was already a little too-too tight—and if I pretended not to notice that when I stretched against the pole of the Z-rod and complained about how much my back hurt, my shirt rose up just enough to make Luke uncomfortable, and his face got red and his hands sweaty—he'd fall all over himself to help me do whatever it was I really didn't want to do. He'd reach out with those hands and touch mine, taking the hangers, the plastic, the clothes from me. "I'll get this," he'd say. "You stretch out your back." And I would. Making sure he could watch.

Luke was a lot safer than Sam.

Sam also made it clear that he thought I was better than normal. Or maybe he thought more along the lines of what Gunner may have thought: *better than nothing.*

Sam would appear like some sort of magician in a puff of smoke (courtesy of the cigarettes that always hung from his lips or between his fingers).

On the Saturday before my sixteenth birthday, I had to work stock with Luke all day long and then race home to eat and change and be substitute *mamma* for two little girls who lived down the street.

Somehow, Luke had learned that the following Thursday was my sweet sixteen. I was lost in my own thoughts, hiding in the very back of the stockroom, absentmindedly stripping clothes of their plastic wraps. Trying to time the rips and the pops of their protective sleeves with the Muzak playing, sort of like adding drums or a beat or life to lifeless tunes. Singing words, either the ones I knew or ones I would make up, ever so softly, but in my head singing them at the top of my lungs. I remember "Sad Eyes" playing. A lot. Muzak even did a decent job with it. I loved that song. Loved hearing my own voice singing it, piercing the silence that suffocated me.

"Thursday's your birthday."

The voice startled me.

I swung around, not recognizing it, then relaxed a bit at the sight of Luke, even though he was more disheveled-looking than usual.

"Hey. Hi. Yeah. My birthday. It is. Thursday."

He looked like Luke, but not exactly. He sounded like Luke, but like he had a cold or something. It was Luke, but something wasn't right.

"Sweet sixteen, right?"

Something was different about Luke that day. His eyes seemed to be darker and more pushed out from their sockets. I had seen those eyes before. They looked like they were trying to reach out to me, ahead of the rest of his face.

I suddenly became aware of where I was. A feeling I had never felt with Luke started to warm my body. It wasn't the jumblies. It was something else. I felt cornered, my back pinned—almost literally—to the wall. I moved my eyes around, instinctively looking for an escape route. And at the same time, I chastised myself for doing so. Why was I feeling this way? This was Luke.

"I'm not going to be here on Thursday, and I didn't want to miss your birthday."

The Muzak seemed to get louder.

Luke advanced toward me. I wanted to take a step back but really didn't have the room, so I just stood there, bracing for what, I didn't know.

"I couldn't sleep last night. I was thinking of you. Sometimes I can't sleep. I take pills to help me sleep."

I froze. Even my breathing seemed to stop. The Muzak started to sound as if it were underwater. Luke's words were coming out more and more slowly, like when a record isn't playing up to speed. Fear— fear of Luke—spread through me.

"Did you hear me? This is for you."

As if a switch had just been flipped, everything was back up to speed and sounded normal again. And Luke stood before me with a gray velvet box in his hands.

"Happy almost sweet sixteen."

I thought about Mamma. I couldn't help it. Anything having to do with anybody popping pills, even aspirin, freaked me out. And given what Luke had just told me, I suddenly wasn't sure whom I had been thinking I was in control of all this time.

"Luke . . ."

"Open it. My mom helped me pick it out."

I breathed, trying to calm myself. I took the box and opened it, and inside was a little silver chain with a tiny cross hanging from it. It sat there, almost twinkling at me, winking at me, calling me names. For a moment, I wondered if this was some sort of message to me from someone other than God. A cross? I thought it was weird. Of all the necklaces he could have been chosen—a butterfly, a flower, a star—why a cross? I felt as if someone was trying to remind me to be good *or* was mocking me, knowing what had happened with Gunner and Father Tierney—knowing that I had sinned and, worse, that I was not absolved of my sins.

I touched it, purposely bringing my wristwatch into view. It was time to go home.

"It's so pretty," I heard myself saying, convincing even myself. But before anything else could come out of my mouth, Luke had both his hands on my upper arms and his mouth pressed up against mine. He caught me by surprise. I didn't move and had to force myself not to start coughing and choking.

It wasn't that I didn't like Luke. I just didn't expect this from him.

I pushed away, not to the point of being rude, but I had to go. I had to make it to my next job.

I could tell from Luke's eyes that he was hurt by my sudden movement, which he interpreted, I'm sure, as rejection. Because it sort of was.

I thanked Luke for his gift and pushed past him, trying not to appear as if I were running.

I had to get out of there.

Luke was safe. I was in charge.

I had to get out of there.

I got home. I pushed open the front door and nearly jumped at the sight of Mamma standing there. Usually I was prepared to see her, wide-eyed, spooked, statue-like, just standing there, waiting for me. But on this day, I was distracted.

She grabbed my arm. I didn't know what she wanted. I never really knew. Sometimes I tried to engage with her and find out. Most of the time I blew right by her, pretending she wasn't even there.

This time was the latter. I yanked my arm free and raced past her and up the stairs to my room. I locked the door behind me, just to be safe. I pulled Luke's gift out of my pocket and hid it under a bunch of T-shirts in one of my drawers. I stripped out of my work clothes and put on my jeans and some top, something kid-friendly and parent-approved. Something that fit and covered me up.

I couldn't think about Luke, about his gift, about my *mamma*, about turning sweet sixteen, about all the things I wanted to think about. I just needed to get myself out of the house and on to the next thing that would take my mind off all the other things.

The moment I stepped outside and took my first breath of outside evening air, I knew he was there. I could smell him. He never let up, begging, walking backward in front of me. From the moment I stepped outside my house to the moment we arrived at whatever house I was scheduled to babysit at, there was Sam Stone.

I had let Sam come babysit with me a few times. I sort of felt like I had no choice. I was already too tired from having to legitimately earn enough money to pay for school and anything else I wanted. It was easier just to say yes to Sam. And at least with Sam, I knew with certainty what he believed me to be saying yes to.

I was still in control of him.

Sam had food with him, McDonald's. I was so hungry; I had eaten, I'm sure, but it was never enough.

"Is that for me?" I asked, already starting down the sidewalk, praying that Mamma wasn't watching from the window. "You know it's my birthday Thursday. Sweet sixteen."

I don't know why I said what I said in the way I said it, other than because I was hungry and wanted whatever he had in that McDonald's bag.

"It's yours if you want it," Sam responded in his usual way. Whatever Sam Stone said seemed to sound as if it were a dare, or some sort of demand, that you beg for whatever he already really wanted to give you. That was just his way.

Then again, maybe he thought that I said things in that kind of way, too. And maybe he was right.

I tried not to think of Gunner's fortieth birthday.

"So it's not my birthday present?"

Sam stopped abruptly, forcing me to stop as well. He puffed dramatically on his cigarette, blowing the smoke up and out into the heavens. His one eye squinted in its usual way, always letting me know when he was lying.

"Give me a little credit, would ya? McDonald's is not an appropriate sweet-sixteen surprise. Especially not for someone as special as you."

I shook my head, not buying a single word of what he'd said. I was no dumb bunny. Still, what he'd said and the way he'd said it made it impossible to suppress a smile. And I knew that only encouraged him.

I pushed past him. Sam followed, getting in front of me and again doing what he always did: turning around to walk backward. He reached into the McDonald's bag, pulled out a pack of french fries, and held them out to me. I didn't want to give in, but I could not resist. I grabbed a few fries, and we kept on walking, Sam finally turning to face the same direction I was.

"You didn't even know it was my birthday."

"True, but now that I do, I'll give you the best birthday present you've ever gotten from a boyfriend."

"You're not my boyfriend." I grabbed more fries.

Stealing was a lot easier and more lucrative than stocking and baby-sitting. No longer did I work weekends only; in order to pay my bills and still afford stuff I wanted, I was pretty much on call twenty-four-seven. It made me the most popular and sought-after babysitter on the block. "Experienced" is what they called me. Sometimes I even had to turn down same-night gigs. I always made sure, however, to "pencil" people in, telling them I couldn't really commit until a couple days prior because I had to put my schoolwork first. They all said they understood. Truth is, it had nothing to do with schoolwork. It had to do with the dads. I always waited to see if the kids with the cuter dads needed my services first. I knew it was wrong, and I never planned on doing anything with those dads, but when they drove me home at night, I could pretend I was with Gunner again.

Sam wasn't Gunner. But sometimes he made me feel the jumblies.

He would linger outside the houses I babysat in until the parents were long gone. He'd try to come in before the kids were for sure asleep. It was a struggle to keep him out until I was sure it was safe to let him in. I needed the money and couldn't afford to lose these babysitting gigs, or to lose my reputation as a good girl who could be trusted to watch somebody else's kids.

I was a good girl. I had to keep reminding myself of that. I hadn't done anything. Anything to warrant otherwise. Had I?

No. I hadn't. I was n-o-r-m-a-l.

I tried to convince myself.

Sam would sit next to me, our thighs touching, on the couch. We'd watch TV together. He'd always insert his own dialogue into the actors' words. Sam's comments were always funnier. Even when they weren't, I just couldn't help but laugh. He made me laugh.

Sam kept bringing up my birthday and kept insinuating the kind of gift he wanted to give me. I was sorry I had said anything about my sweet sixteen. I let him kiss me. Sam's kiss wasn't anything like Luke's, but Luke had surprised me, so that really wasn't fair. I tried not to think of Gunner—his smile, the strawberry frosting around his mouth, the taste of his tongue . . .

I shot up from the couch, realizing Sam's hand had started making its way down the front of my pants, though they were still zipped and buttoned. I stood, a little wobbly, and had to shake Gunner from my brain before I could clearly see Sam looking up at me, his hair a bit damp, his eyes raised to the ceiling in frustration.

I made Sam leave. I told him it was too late; the parents would be home any second. He didn't argue. He didn't push. As much as Sam was pushy, he knew when to back off. He left—pissed off, I could tell. But I knew he'd be back. He hadn't yet gotten what he wanted. And I realized that people don't leave until they have what they came for, whether you give it freely or not.

I stood outside my own front door. I knew Papà would be home; he always waited up for me. And with him there, I knew, Mamma would be elsewhere, most likely in her room or downstairs stewing. She would not be waiting for me behind the front door. Not when Papà was home. And she usually didn't start her midnight rants until Papà went to bed.

I tried to stay up as late as I could with my *papà*. I wished he would not sleep in the same bed with Mamma. We all knew that she still had knives between the mattress and the springboard. We all knew that she kept baseball bats underneath the bed. We all knew that she had every intention, all the strength she needed, and an overabundance of craziness to carry out her threats of killing Papà in his sleep. The medications really didn't help. I was pretty sure she wasn't even taking them. The longer I could keep him awake, the safer he was.

The moment he heard me enter, he would rise from his chair at the kitchen table and greet me halfway down the hall. He'd ask me how my day was. He'd ask me if I was hungry, if I had eaten. And without fail, Papà and I would spend another hour, at least, catching up while sharing some treat and possibly working on some problem that needed solving—some bill we could not pay, some teacher's meeting he could not make, some something that mattered.

Papà was in an extra-special good mood that night. "*Sedici anni fa, è nata la più perfetta bimba, Paolamia! Come celebreremo?*"

I did not feel like the most perfect baby to have been born sixteen years ago. Maybe I was back then, but keeping up, trying to stay that perfect Paolina, was killing me. How could I tell him that I didn't want to celebrate my sweet sixteen? I couldn't. So I avoided answering. Instead, I told him I had something to show him. I dashed to my bedroom, retrieved Luke's gift, and brought it back downstairs.

I showed the tiny cross to my *papà*. I told him what had happened that day with Luke. All of it. I then told him what had happened that night with Sam. Most of it. I spoke so softly, in barely a whisper, sometimes whispering directly into Papà's ear, for fear that Mamma was listening and I would find myself in hot water as soon as she and I were alone.

Papà listened, without interrupting. At times, when I told him about Luke, he sort of seemed like he was trying to hold in his laughter. And when I told him about Sam, his eyebrows kept going up, and sometimes he shut his eyes and sort of sucked in his lips.

I waited to hear my *papà*'s words. I wanted to know what he thought of it all. I needed to be told what to do.

Papà touched the tiny cross necklace, saying how nice it was, how it meant a lot for a boy to give a girl a gift, especially like this. And if I accepted the gift, it would mean even more to a boy who would give a gift like that. So I had to make sure it meant just as much to me.

He then told me that the next time Sam came around, he wanted to meet him. He made sure I promised to introduce them before I did any more babysitting with Sam.

I promised, not really sure I would keep my promise.

Papà rose from his chair. I could tell he was exhausted. I was, too. He kissed me good night on the forehead. His right hand, so big and leathery and warm, caressed my cheek. I so wanted to fall into that hand, to close my eyes and fall asleep.

As he pushed in his chair and turned to make his way to bed, he stopped and stared at me. I couldn't quite make out the look on his face. It was half like he was bursting with pride, like when I'd told him I had gotten a better job, at Marshall Field's, and half like he was going to cry, like when I'd told him that I had gotten Gunner to say yes to helping us put Mamma in the hospital. He put his hand on my shoulder and leaned over to whisper in my ear words I can still hear as clearly as if he were standing by me, saying them now:

"Paolamia, ricordarti: qualunque ragazzo con cui tu vai, è a chi dài il tuo cuore, promettimi che tieni per te stesso sempre un piccolo pezzo; non mai dare tutto il tuo cuore a nessuno. Promettermi?"

I looked into my *papà*'s eyes and promised: no matter what boy I ended up with, no matter to whom I ended up giving my heart, I promised never to give all of it, but always to keep a little piece of my heart only for me.

I promised, knowing that this was a promise I would keep.

Suicide

I hid the little box, the one that held the necklace with the tiny cross in it, in my pocket. In the darkened stockroom at Marshall Field's, I stripped plastic off the latest collections, readying them for their shopping debuts.

Luke came to me. He made a move as if wanting to kiss me. It took me by surprise, given how I reacted the first time. I figured either he was more persistent than I gave him credit for being, or he was just slow.

I stepped back. Not out of fear, but because I chose not to be kissed.

He looked a bit confused. I didn't want to hurt him, but I didn't want there to be any more confusion. I pulled his gift out of my pocket and held it out to him.

"I can't take this, Luke."

"Why?"

I thought about how much I wanted to ask Gunner that very question. So tiny, yet so powerful. Why? I wanted an answer from him. Just as Luke wanted one from me.

I wondered if Gunner kept his distance because he didn't want to be asked the question, didn't want to have to answer it.

Just as I really didn't want to now.

I don't remember what answer I even gave to Luke. I just remember his eyes. How those brown eyes welled up with tears, turning red-rimmed. He tried to make me keep the necklace. I refused. Finally he took it from me, turning away and disappearing.

I felt worse turning down Luke than I did about Sam. I also don't remember what words I used to make Sam go away. I know only that I did. And that Sam would try for a while to keep coming back, not taking me at my word.

It didn't matter, though. Because I kept clear in my message to him. Pretty much one word, constantly one word: "no."

It finally worked. Sam didn't come around any longer.

In a way I had not felt since I couldn't remember when, I was more free, powerful, more in control of everybody—most of all me.

And that lasted for a while.

Until I lost control.

I don't know what sparked it.

The day I chose to kill my *mamma*.

I'm not even sure I "chose" to do it. It just sort of happened.

It started out a normal-as-normal-could-be-in-a-crazy-house-hold kind of day. As usual, it was my job to fix Mamma's coffee before I left the house for school. I was sweet sixteen, but in truth, any possibility of sweetness in me had been abandoned long ago. So much had happened to me, and I believed I had one person to blame: Mamma. Or maybe the only person I had to blame was me. I wasn't sure at that point, nor am I sure now.

In truth, I don't think I really planned it. I think, had I been prosecuted, they would have been hard pressed to confirm it was premeditated. I simply had had enough. I had gotten an idea. I realized no one would know. And I acted upon it. Is that "premed-itated"? I don't know, and fortunately—or not—I would not find out. Not this time. Because I failed. Miserably. And that may have been worse than succeeding. To live with knowing that someone knows you want to kill her is worse than actually doing or having done it.

Mamma liked a little coffee with her sugar. For some reason, on this particular day, I opened up the cupboard, pulled out Mamma's favorite coffee cup, slid open a drawer, pulled out a spoon, slid it shut, and waited until the coffee snorted out its last perc. I watched the clock. I was running late. I could barely keep my eyes open. *Did I do my algebra homework? Did I finish my essay?* My mind raced and at the same time refused to move.

My eyes focused inside the cupboard; all the bottles of Mamma's prescription medicines zoomed into view. Prolixin. Cogentin. Haldol. Chlorpromazine. Lithium. Stelazine. So many names of antipsychotic and mood-stabilizing drugs known to me throughout the years. I don't remember how many or which ones, exactly, my mother was taking in the early 1980s. But I do remember Prolixin and chlorpromazine: my introduction into the power of prescriptions. And the base for my poisonous potion.

As if not in control of my extremities, I pulled down all the bottles. I pulled a knife out from the drawer. I split open each capsule. I poured contents into the cup. I smashed up whole, solid pills until they became a fine powder. I laced Mamma's coffee with whatever she had, at least enough of a concoction that would prove, hopefully, to be lethal.

I wanted her gone.

I loaded in the sugar. I poured in a splash of milk and the espresso-strength coffee. I always tasted Mamma's coffee before bringing it to her. I wanted to make sure it was just the way she liked it. I nearly did the same on this day. Wouldn't that have proved it really wasn't premeditated? Or maybe the fact that I stopped short of taking a sip proved otherwise. What I do know is that the counter was sprinkled with evidence of powders that did not belong. And I also know that I did not care. *That* surely would have pointed to its not being premeditated.

I picked up the teaspoon and swirled my concoction. Tapping the spoon on the side of the cup, I then rested it on the counter and, with full coffee cup in hand, turned to carry it to Mamma.

Half a spin, and I was face-to-face with her. Without any warning, any sound, there she was. There she had been. Watching me. Watching me throughout my entire pharmaceutical experience. Saying not a word. Just watching. I recoiled ever so slightly. Our eyes squared off.

"*Paoletta?*" She barely whispered it.

Questioning. This diminutive, childlike version of my name: "Little Paolina."

It should have been endearing. Instead, it sounded damning. Accompanied by the look in her eyes, she needed not say more. It was clear.

She knew.

I knew.

We both knew.

She had been watching as I sliced open pills and poured them into her cup. She had watched it all. In silence.

To this day, I wonder what she must have thought. Or maybe what she thought, she had thought all along. Maybe it would not have mattered had I done it, had I been caught, had I succeeded, had I done nothing. Maybe, like Judas, I was just fulfilling my fate, what she already thought of me. What she already knew me to be. Who I really was.

I struggled to shrug off the schizophrenic strain I had come to fear lay within me. I pretended it wasn't happening. At the same time, another part of me prayed I'd find the courage to finish what I had started.

Mamma extended her hand to me. Without taking her eyes from mine, she reached for the cup. Her cup. Filled with what she thought might end the torturous life she had come to know.

Her action confused me.

Was this a selfless act by my *mamma*, ready to give up her life, give me what I want, because even she thought it'd be best for her daughter? Or was this simply another act of craziness? Did she know? I no longer did.

"Ma." I could choke out nothing more.

Whether on purpose or by accident, I let the cup slip from my fingers. It crashed to the floor. I looked at it. I looked at her. Her eyes. God, her eyes—round and black, a void of wild terror. As afraid as I had become now of years more with my *mamma*, her eyes told me at that moment just how afraid she was of me. Of *me*?

I suddenly snapped to. Me. Me. Afraid of monster me.

I was who she thought me to be.

I needed to get out of there. Now.

I practically shoved her out of the way. I had meant to step over the broken china and the puddle of poison pooling on the floor, but in my haste I stepped right on top of it all, tracking evidence from the kitchen through the hallway to the front door, where I grabbed my book bag and my keys and pushed out the door. I shut my ears and my eyes, focusing on my escape. But I could not help but hear her soft whimpers calling my name.

I jammed the key into the car door's lock. My first car, bought and paid for by me: $2,500 cash. I had started campaigning for a car the moment I turned fifteen. "Three things I know I don't want, Papà: a car that's white, a stick shift, and a sunroof that was put in after the car was actually made." Man makes plans; God laughs, goes the saying. The moment I turned sixteen, in 1981, there by the side of the road sat my baby, a FOR SALE sign affixed to her window. Three things she was: a white Ford Escort, a stick shift, with an after-factory sunroof that would leak whenever it rained. Papà reminded me that this wasn't what I wanted and that we should keep looking. But the heart wants what the heart wants. And something inside me knew that she was the one and I had to have her.

As the engine roared on the morning I tried to poison Mamma, the radio came to life, and I knew from the words of the song that played that God had decided once again to speak to me.

I have no idea, no memory of how I drove from my home to our church. Did I run any red lights? Did I run anybody over? I remember only being surrounded by that song, the words of it escorting me on my journey. I had never heard it before. I would learn its name, "Under Pressure," by Queen and David Bowie, later. But from the moment we were introduced, I knew the words being sung were a message from God about insanity and cracking under pressure and giving ourselves one more chance.

I sat in my car in the parking lot outside St. Peter's, though I have no idea why I went there.

I half sung—more like murmured—the words over and over in my head. I looked over at the church. I started sort of laughing. But at the same time was sort of crying.

I realized I could not go in and ask forgiveness. But at the same time, only God knows why, I also realized that I did not need to.

"Under Pressure" became my theme song. In moments of fear or doubt or shame, I would recite its words, sing its tune, silently, deep inside. To myself. Still do.

No one really means to hurt anyone else. Do they? I didn't. I believe my *papà* didn't. I am pretty sure Mamma didn't. Did Mrs. Regan? Did Gunner? Is it possible no one really means to hurt anyone else? It's just pressure? Or am I that naive? I wanted my *mamma—my own mother*—dead. Who was I? What did that make me? How could I condemn others who had hurt me? How could I not forgive them? How would I ever forgive myself?

I came to understand how people can be pushed to their limits to do things they would never think they would do, not in a million years. I myself never thought I would do what I did. Never. In a million years or beyond. But I had been pushed to my limit.

I made it to school that day, though I don't remember much of anything that happened there, except the other raging battle in my life, which revolved around my going away to college.

One woman was championing the idea with such fervor that I couldn't help but wonder if she was simply another kind of crazy. She just wouldn't let it go.

"Carrie Cabot College Counselor."

That's how she introduced herself. In a singsongy kind of way. Not just the first time you met her, but every single time after that. At first I thought it was because she had a bad memory. Then I thought it was because I just wasn't that memorable. But soon, I realized it was just who she was and how she spoke.

I wasn't exactly a fan of hers, for a lot of reasons—first and foremost, the way she greeted you with that "Carrie Cabot . . ." line. Drove me nuts. I had to stop myself from cutting her off at the first "C." But it was more than that. When it came down to it, she just didn't get it. She didn't get the fact that I wasn't going away to college, no matter what scholarships or other money she could find for me.

I tried to explain to her that I definitely *was* going to college, but that I couldn't leave home, couldn't leave my *papà* especially, without explaining the why of it to her. But no matter how hard I tried to tell her, without really telling her, she just wasn't listening. And the more she didn't listen, the more I had to hear about all the faraway, great-sounding, all-about-me schools that were "dying to have me." And the more that I was forced to listen, the more it hurt to hear about everything I knew I had to let go.

"Bradley University is flying out to see *you* about a scholarship to its School of Engineering program," she said, sitting on the edge of her desk, her arms outstretched, her hands on my shoulders, as I sat in a nearby chair, wishing I could disappear.

We had all been given some aptitude-analysis tests, which included basic English and algebra exam questions and, in addition, asked a bunch of questions about what we liked to do and questions that were more like riddles or puzzles to be solved. Girls had been talking in the halls about how those tests were going to determine whether you would become a janitor or a judge after graduation. I knew I didn't want to be a janitor, but beyond that, I dreamed of being a lawyer or a vet or an obstetrician. I knew I wanted to be somebody. But to be that somebody, I knew I couldn't leave home.

It didn't really matter anyway. I didn't have a choice—no one did—about taking the tests, so I took them. Had I given it some thought, however, I would have not answered correctly, truthfully. I could have blown it on purpose. Should have.

Not having choices sometimes seemed easier.

I could see in Carrie Cabot's eyes that she just couldn't understand why I wasn't as excited as she was. But I couldn't be.

I wondered if she could see in my eyes how much this was killing me.

Did she really think I did not want to jump up and down and tell the world that I'd aced those tests? That I had been chosen? Who cared if it was for engineering? Who the hell wants to be an engineer? I didn't even really know what an engineer did, but I knew it wasn't as important to me as being a doctor or a lawyer.

But the chance to get away, to be by myself, to be free—*that* was something I wished for more than anyone could possibly understand.

"Miss Cabot, I know this is a really good thing, but I just don't think it's for me." I said it as I had said it numerous times before, regardless of what college counseling came my way, knowing full well my words would fall on deaf ears.

Carrie Cabot stood tall, arching her back and breathing in loudly. She did that every time we met. I knew she was frustrated. So was I.

She rounded her desk, sat back down in her chair, picked up a pencil, scribbled something onto her desk calendar, looked up at me, and smiled, as if the last few minutes of exasperation had never happened.

"They'll be here next week. And so will you. And your parents." She paused for a few seconds, looking at me. Almost as if she were studying me. Then she sort of shook her head, ever so slightly, and said, "It never hurts to talk, Paolina. And that's what we'll do."

She didn't really give me an opportunity to respond. I was still slow in finding my voice. And she already had her head down and was thumbing through other manila folders filled with whatever was now more worthy than I was. Had she waited just a second more before dismissing me, maybe I would have told her what I was thinking, what my insides were screaming at me to say: *"Carrie Cabot College Counselor, you are so wrong, on all counts."*

Bradley University might show up, but I wouldn't be there. And neither would my parents. And it does hurt to talk. Especially when the words aren't what you want to hear, and when what you really want to say needs to remain secret.

I dreaded going home. Facing Mamma.

But I had no choice.

School had ended for the day.

I wasn't on the schedule at work.

I had no babysitting gigs lined up for that evening.

I feared what I would find.

"Paoletta?"

I feared her.

I feared myself.

"Not hereditary." That's what the doctors told my family, back when I was in high school. But I was smart enough to know that the very medical profession that would cut open my mother's brain to poke around and see what there was to see didn't have all the answers—especially considering how much worse it got after surgery. I had also learned to doubt pretty much everything and everyone by then, especially so-called authority figures. Mistrustful me was actually quite confident that most docs didn't even know the questions. So I set out to find both.

E-x-p-l-o-r-a-t-i-o-n consumed me.

I needed to silence the voices inside me, the ones that kept whispering what a carbon copy of my *mamma* I was. I needed to know what "it" was that tormented her. I needed to fill the holes and find out for myself: brain disorders, abnormalities, drug treatments, mental illness, heredity factors.

Like a treasure hunt. One clue led to another.

Something inside me already knew that "it" *was* hereditary. I didn't really need to crack a book. I had thought long ago that Mamma's stories of how her own aunts were visited by "spirits" were just that: stories. But now, looking even at the photos of my grandmother and her haunting eyes (the same eyes my mother and even my younger sister had), I knew. I did not know exactly what "it" was called; it didn't matter what its name was.

I just needed to make sure that "it" did not choose to choose me. I needed to control my growing fears that I had not fallen far enough from the family tree.

My research resulted in a timeline. I read that thirty was the magical age, the threshold, that seemed to mark the end of "it" being able to possess you. I would have to wait, wonder, and wish; I would have to reach 1995, more than a decade away, to be able to proclaim myself finally free.

Please, God, don't let it be me.

I entered through the front door and looked at my surroundings. I didn't know whether to expect the mess I had left to still be there or not.

What I found could be summed up in one word: "immaculate."

It's the only word that comes to mind.

The foyer, the hallway, the kitchen, all of it had been scrubbed clean. All evidence of what I had done or tried to do had vanished.

No sign of Mamma, either.

I didn't seek her out. I made my way through the house, resting my book bag on the floor, against the wall, under the phone that hung there in the kitchen.

I don't know how long it took, but I know that Papà had come home, so it must have been somewhere around dinnertime. I know that he asked me where Mamma was. Dinner was not on the table. It wasn't even on the stove or in the oven.

I know I apologized to Papà, opening doors to cabinets and the refrigerator to see what we might eat.

He called out to Mamma, asking her what we should eat.

"Maria? Marietta . . . ? Che mangiamo?"

I then heard Papà sort of gasp. I turned to see a disheveled Mamma sort of stumble out of her bedroom door at the top of the stairs, just as Viny emerged from her adjacent room.

Mamma held her throat or, alternately, her chest with one hand. Her eyes were panicked. I could barely understand her slurred words, until I heard her say, *"Ambulanza!"*

Papà immediately sprang into action, climbing the stairs, just as she started to fall.

My eyes connected with Viny's, as she stood now just behind and to the side of Mamma. Viny shut her eyes slowly, tilting her head back a little. I could see her chin quivering as she backed up into her bedroom, closing the door behind her.

Mamma was taken to the hospital.

I wondered that day, as I have wondered almost every day since then, if her attempt at suicide was simply her attempt to carry out what she and I both knew I had started. I wondered if what she had so meticulously cleaned up that day was, indeed, what she had somehow salvaged and, perhaps, taken. I wondered if this, again, was all because of me.

I wanted to tell her how sorry I was. I wanted to ask for her forgiveness.

But I never did.

And she never spoke a word about any of it to me or anybody else.

From November 19 to December 5, 1981, Mamma and Papà took up residence at St. Luke's Hospital in Pittsburgh, where doctors renowned for their expertise in neurological disorders agreed to perform another surgery on my *mamma*'s head.

Once again, I stepped up my role as *la piccola mamma*; once again, we entertained possibilities beyond the psychological; once again, I danced upon self-doubt and swallowed calories upon calories of self-loathing and silence; once again, we repeated never-ending cycles of sickness and screaming and drama and secrets.

Never-ending.

And I was sick of it.

Survival

"Sticks and stones may break my bones, but words will never hurt me."

What a lie.

Words wound.

They torture.

They kill.

The ones my mother heard in her head—warning her we were out to kill her, whispering to her to kill us or be killed, convincing her to attempt to kill herself—were proof.

Other words, other voices were equally powerful.

Gunner's:

"Help me with my pussy problem."

"Six of one, half dozen of another. Now we're even."

Father Tierney's:

"I cannot absolve you of your sins."

So many voices. So many words.

And the ones I used in my own moments of rage devastated.

"Because I don't want to end up like you!"

I didn't really mean it. Or at least not the way the words came out.

Not the way they sliced through my father's heart, splintering his weathered face, exposing even more cracks in his Roman facade.

His silence.

His resignation.

His defeat.

"Okay, Paola. You go 'way to *la scuola*."

His words gave me permission to go away to school. His eyes turned glassy, apologizing for failing, for being human.

I hated myself. As much as I internally celebrated my victory, applauded myself for finding my voice, standing up for myself, saving whatever normalcy was left in me, and getting what I wanted, I hated myself.

"*Papà, non volevo dire . . .*" I tried to tell him I hadn't meant to say what I'd said. But it was too late. The words were out, the damage done. And the voice was mine.

I just couldn't do it any longer. I could not stay where so much had happened to me, around me, and yet nothing was really for me.

I didn't mean that I didn't want to be like him. I meant I didn't want to end up struggling from paycheck to paycheck, having to give up what I loved to do, having to work two jobs—one in a factory, packing cans of soup, and another washing floors after-hours in a Kmart—just to survive. I didn't want to sacrifice myself for someone else who could not be saved.

I remember the closing of the barbershop my *papà* owned and loved. The sale of the fancy cash register was the final sign that it was over. As my father shined up its brass scrolls, taking care to clean each individual numbered lever, tears formed in the corners of his eyes. He took his white handkerchief, the one my mother had embroidered with his initials, from his pants pocket and blew his nose. He saw me watching him. He wanted to say something. He licked his lips and swallowed a few times. But no words came out. Instead he nodded and winked at me. Then he turned back to finish readying the antique that had been handed down to him by his father and his father's father—a family heirloom that had followed him all the way from Italy when he'd first come to the United States with the hope of making his millions—knowing that his American dreams were now over.

We needed the money from the sale just to make ends meet. It had come to this: selling off bits and pieces of things that were more than just things, pretending they meant nothing.

Pretending gets easier with practice.

And I had pretended for months. Months that stretched into years. Watching friends leave for out-of-state colleges. Wishing them well. Commuting almost daily to my inner-city school. Working my job. Paying bills. Coming home to crazy, trying to take care of my family. Trying to forget people who should be forgotten. Trying to stay safe. Soothing myself with food. Keeping secrets. And exhausting myself to make sure nobody on the outside really knew what was still going on.

Secrets are harder to keep when you're exhausted.

I was now a sophomore at the University of Illinois at Chicago. It wasn't a bad school. But it was an at-home school.

For years now, in secret, every chance I'd gotten, I'd filled out applications to schools far away. Going to college was a way out of where I was. And I could do it with free money. Scholarships. At least enough for one year.

And that's all I was asking for. Just one year.

Letters from those schools would come in the mail—some of them thin, some of them fat. All of them ended up in the garbage, unopened.

I wanted to leave. I did. I wanted to be free. But for the longest time, I couldn't make myself take that leap.

I told myself it was because of my family. I told myself that I just couldn't leave my *papà* alone to deal. With every discarded letter, I pretended that, in part, it wasn't me. I wasn't the reason that I wasn't leaving. I pretended because inside I had convinced myself that existing in my unstable world was in so many ways safer, easier to navigate, more fulfilling in terms of purpose, than living among "normal" and living just for me could ever be.

I deserved the life I was leading.

That is what I believed.

But somewhere deep inside me, I must not have. Not fully. If I had, I wouldn't have kept filling out college applications. Even if I sometimes never mailed them, even if I destroyed responses that came to the ones I did, some part of me must have known that the day would come when one response would survive and I would finally force myself to move.

That day came.

I had just gotten home—from where, I don't recall. As usual, I pulled the letters out of our mailbox. No one else in the family seemed to care about collecting it. So I just added it to my other daily duties.

Bills. Flyers. Junk.

And an envelope from Iowa State University. It was a school I knew little about. I had applied only because Ross had managed to escape to it the year prior, just for the year. Originally, we had hatched a secret plan to go together, but at the last minute, I'd chickened out. I had not been able to shake thoughts of how my going would give Mamma further fodder for the thoughts she harbored about my brother and me.

I stood there, the front door unopened, only then noticing the screams coming from inside my home.

I pushed on the door. It slowly swung open to reveal my younger sister, Viny, on the ground in a fetal position, her hands trying to cover her head, protecting herself from Mamma's blows. Ranting, raving, piercing with that shrill, uncontrolled screaming about something real or imagined, Mamma raged at her youngest daughter.

While Viny uttered not a sound.

I froze for barely a moment. To intervene could prove painful. Not to wasn't an option.

I raced toward Mamma, threw my arms around hers to render her incapable of striking again, and shouted, "Enough! Enough!"

But I was shouting more to myself.

And this time I heard me.

The August day in 1985 when Papà and I left at dawn for Iowa State University, six hours away, just he and I driving alone on Route 30, couldn't have been more like midwestern summer: sun already scorching at sunrise, hazy skies with showers of parachuting white dandelion puffs, plumes of steam rising from black-tarred roads, the smell of fresh manure. We could have taken Interstate 80, but then we would have missed the rural countryside we both loved: cows, horses, barns, rows upon rows of corn—earthy, simple things that mattered just by being.

I don't remember what we talked about. I don't remember if we sat silently, staring straight ahead, but I doubt that was the case. I imagine we pointed out livestock and barn construction and field colors. I imagine we stopped to pee and to fill empty gas tanks and tummies at truck stops and diners.

I do remember our arrival on campus grounds. Students directed us, our U-Haul, to the appropriate drop-off area. We pulled out boxes and lugged them to my appointed room: a kitchenette with nothing more than two cots.

Temporary housing, they called it. I had committed so late to attending that there wasn't an available room for me, so until something opened up (I assumed that meant some other student would quit or be kicked out), this windowless cell was to be my home.

I could read it on my *papà*'s face: *This is where you'd rather live than your own home?*

What I hoped he could not read on mine was my answer: *Yes.*

By early afternoon, we were finished. It was time for us to part ways.

Papà wasn't ready.

It wasn't that he didn't want me to go away to college, to experience life on my own, to realize my dreams, to be free. I think that his not wanting me to go away had more to do with his fear that he wouldn't make it without me. And that made him no different from any other parent, any other anybody, under normal circumstances, let alone what ours had become.

I understood. And while I knew I, too, would miss him terribly, and while, no, I didn't love the idea of sleeping on a cot in a window-less kitchenette with a roommate I had never met before, and while, yes, I was scared to death . . .

It was what *I* needed for me.

We walked around the campus for a while.

"*E quando ritorni, che farai?*" Papà already wanted to know what I would be when I returned.

I shrugged my shoulders. I could not think yet of having to return. I had only enough scholarship money and loans to get me through midyear; I had yet to even get a job to pay for the rest. I could not think about it. So I did not answer but asked him a question in return.

"*Se potresti farlo di nuovo, che diventaresti?*" I had never asked him before. And I wanted to know: If he could do it all over again, what would he have become?

Now Papà shrugged his shoulders. A dozen possibilities played out across his face. He had done more in his life than so many others twice his age, with at least that much more in opportunities. He'd never made it beyond the third grade, yet he was wiser than most with graduate degrees. He had lived on three continents, and really *lived*, learning the languages and musical instruments, becoming one of the locals. He'd learned to tailor clothes, cook meals, style hair, and built his own business in a foreign country, not yet knowing the English language. He had escaped living the life of a Mafioso, putting his own life in jeopardy for refusing to marry a mobster's daughter. He had raised a family of six, managed as best he could, with a wife who was the victim of a fairly unknown mental illness, on an annual salary of no more than $25,000. He owned a home and wasn't even in debt.

And yet, without meaning to, I had succeeded in making him feel like a failure.

Words wound.

"*Forse un architetto.*"

An architect. I could see him creating, building things.

"*Papà* . . ." I wanted to tell him, say the words he deserved to hear.

"*O pure un babbo!*"

His blurting out his other choice for what he would become—the word that in Italian means both a clown or buffoon *and* a father—had us both howling with laughter. Papà was wise, indeed, and I knew he knew what my words couldn't yet say.

We ended up in front of the town's movie theater. For the first time in our lives, Papà and I went to watch an afternoon movie together: *Silverado.* I don't think we had any idea what it was about. We both loved westerns, and this story about four misfits who band together and gunfight it out to save a town from the bad guys, starring some of our favorite actors, including Kevin Kline, Kevin Costner, and Brian Dennehy, was our kind of story.

I watched my *papà*'s face light up, the corners of his eyes crinkle with laughter, his toothless grin wide open in awe at the scenes flashing across that magical screen. I felt in that moment all the love and belonging I had experienced as a little girl the first time I fell in love with great stories on the silver screen, sitting with my Uncle Joe, watching *Chitty Chitty Bang Bang* and *Willy Wonka*, as well as all the jumbly feelings I felt as a preteen, falling in love for the first time with Sylvester Stallone and the story of Rocky.

At that moment, I knew we would never be the same—for better and for worse. I was choosing to break free, to be just me. I knew it. And so did he.

He looked over at me looking at him. He took my hand and kissed it. He nodded and winked and turned back to watch the movie.

When it was over, we stepped outside and stood beside our car, along a white picket-like fence that outlined the perimeter of the gravel parking lot. The sun was starting to set, the heat starting to lessen, thanks to a brief rain shower now ending, giving us just a bit of relief. Papà had to get on the road. To get back home. To let me get back to what was now, at least for that year, my new home.

I don't remember what our last words were. I would imagine he said his usual: "*Ti raccomando.*" In translation, the words really just mean, "I recommend," but when Papà said it, it meant so much more, everything from "pay attention" to "be careful" to "I'm watching you, even when you think I'm not" to "I'm always here if you need me" to "I'll never leave you." I'm sure we said "I love you" to each other.

While I can't recall the words, I do recall the visual: a rainbow in the sky. And not just any rainbow, but one vibrant in its colors and of which we could see both ends, touching down on either side of us. We had never seen that before. And my *papà* and I just looked at each other. Words weren't necessary. Lyrics weren't needed. The message was loud and clear. And it wasn't a secret.

Acknowledgments

"*When are you going to stop wishing for a better past?*" The day I did is the day the me I am today finally came to be. And for that, I thank Lynn, the lady who challenged me with those words, and without whom I very well might be six feet under. To the others in my life—family, friends, colleagues, and random run-ins—you are too many to name, and I'd hate to accidentally leave one of you out. I hope you know who you are and just how important you are to me. I thank you all, and I thank the Universe that put you in my path, and that always seems to deliver exactly what I need when I really need it.

About the Author

© Richard Petrillo

For a long time, Paolina has told other people's stories: as a features reporter for a daily newspaper; as a PR pro for a university; as a content marketer for the unsung heroes of small business; and most recently as a storyteller for a nonprofit that funds research to end childhood cancer. She has won awards for her creative marketing and advertising, her fiction pieces and screenplays. *The S-Word* is her first full-length book.

SELECTED TITLES FROM SHE WRITES PRESS

She Writes Press is an independent publishing company
founded to serve women writers everywhere.
Visit us at www.shewritespress.com.

The Coconut Latitudes: Secrets, Storms, and Survival in the Caribbean
by Rita Gardner $16.95, 978-1-63152-901-6
A haunting, lyrical memoir about a dysfunctional family's experiences in a reality far from the envisioned Eden—and the terrible cost of keeping secrets.

A Different Kind of Same: A Memoir by Kelley Clink
$16.95, 978-1-63152-999-3
Several years before Kelley Clink's brother hanged himself, she attempted suicide by overdose. In the aftermath of his death, she traces the evolution of both their illnesses, and wonders: If he couldn't make it, what hope is there for her?

Don't Leave Yet: How My Mother's Alzheimer's Opened My Heart by Constance Hanstedt $16.95, 978-1-63152-952-8
The chronicle of Hanstedt's journey toward independence, self-assurance, and connectedness as she cares for her mother, who is rapidly losing her own identity to the early stage of Alzheimer's.

Her Beautiful Brain: A Memoir by Ann Hedreen
$16.95, 978-1-938314-92-6
The heartbreaking story of a daughter's experiences as her beautiful, brainy mother begins to lose her mind to an unforgiving disease: Alzheimer's.

Say It Out Loud: Revealing and Healing the Scars of Sexual Abuse by Roberta Dolan $16.95, 978-1-938314-99-5
An in-depth guide to healing the wounds caused by sexual abuse, written by a survivor who's lived the process firsthand.

The Rooms Are Filled by Jessica Null Vealitzek
$16.95, 978-1-938314-58-2
The coming-of-age story of two outcasts—a nine-year-old boy who just lost his father, and a closeted young woman—brought together by circumstance.

CPSIA information can be obtained
at www.ICGtesting.com
Printed in the USA
FSOW01n1021050215
5037FS